MW01075177

"Molly DeFrank shows mo[] risks, can laugh through str[] world adventures. Packed w[] this book is your secret weapon for raising bold, resilient, and joyful sons in a world that needs them."

Ginny Yurich, bestselling author, podcaster, and founder of 1000 Hours Outside

"The mom huddle I needed. As a fellow mom wanting to intentionally build up my son in the Lord, I ate up all of Molly's words as she broke down eight critical areas to cultivate, both in his soul and in our mother-son relationship (in a non-boring way, PTL). Chock-full of truth, stats, and encouragement, this is what I call a must-read!"

Heidi Lee Anderson, social media influencer @HeidiLeeAnderson and author of *P.S. It's Gonna Be Good*

"Molly DeFrank is the BFF every mom raising boys needs. *Mothering Boys* gives us her encouraging and godly wisdom with heaps of humor so we can embrace the unique challenges of raising sons in an ever-challenging culture. You'll want to gift a copy to all your boy-mom friends!"

Amber Lia, who lives in a testoster-HOME of four sons with her husband and is the bestselling author or coauthor of multiple books, including *Triggers: Exchanging Parents' Angry Reactions for Gentle Biblical Responses* and *Parenting Scripts*

"As a boy mom to four energetic sons, I know firsthand the challenges and joys of raising boys. This book is a refreshing blend of humor and biblical truth, offering real-life examples that make practical parenting feel achievable, from navigating their failures to encouraging them to get outside—and making those tough conversations easier. I can't recommend this book enough!"

Mikella Van Dyke, author of *Chasing Sacred: Learn How to Study Scripture to Pursue God and Find Hope in Him*

"*Mothering Boys* is exactly the road map I need as I raise my three boys in today's world. With humor and grace, and backed by cutting-edge research, Molly gives practical examples of how to instill character and godly values to the next generation of men. If you have boys, this is a must-read!"

Katie Emma Cook, licensed marriage and family therapist, mother of three boys, blogger, and speaker

MOTHERING
BOYS

Books by Molly DeFrank

Digital Detox
Mothering Boys

MOTHERING
BOYS

8 THINGS YOUR SON NEEDS FROM YOU
BEFORE HE TURNS 10

MOLLY DeFRANK

BETHANYHOUSE

a division of Baker Publishing Group
Minneapolis, Minnesota

Published by Bethany House Publishers
Minneapolis, Minnesota
BethanyHouse.com

Bethany House Publishers is a division of
Baker Publishing Group, Grand Rapids, Michigan

Printed in the United States of America

Library of Congress Cataloging-in-Publication Data
Names: DeFrank, Molly, author.
Title: Mothering boys : 8 things your son needs from you before he turns 10 / Molly DeFrank.
Description: Minneapolis : Bethany House Publishers, a division of Baker Publishing Group, 2025. | Includes bibliographical references.
Identifiers: LCCN 2024041233 | ISBN 9780764243684 (paperback) | ISBN 9780764244988 | ISBN 9781493450756 (ebook)
Subjects: LCSH: Mothers and sons—Religious aspects—Christianity. | Parenting—Religious aspects—Christianity.
Classification: LCC BV4529.18 .D44 2025 | DDC 248.8/45—dc23/eng/20241123
LC record available at https://lccn.loc.gov/2024041233

Published in association with Books & Such Literary Management, BooksAndSuch.com.

Baker Publishing Group publications use paper produced from sustainable forestry practices and postconsumer waste whenever possible.

25 26 27 28 29 30 31   7 6 5 4 3 2 1

To Jack, Carter, and Mason.
I'm forever grateful that you wonderful humans
made me a boy mom.

Picturing my children's hearts as treasure chests where they could gather stories, ideas, ideals, habits, appetites, truth, and knowledge to draw from the rest of their lives, I sought to fill the space in their hearts with all that was good, beautiful, and true. Filling a treasure chest, of course, takes lots of time and intentionality. But I found that my soul became rich in the process.

—Sally Clarkson, *Awaking Wonder*

CONTENTS

Introduction 11

#1 BELONGING 19

1. Value—*More Than Many Sparrows* 21
2. Purpose—*Parents, the Original Strength Finder* 29
3. Family Dinner—*Chaotic, Delicious, Life-Changing* 39

#2 RELATIONSHIP 45

4. Eye Contact—*Peep the Window to the Soul* 47
5. Conversation—*A Tool to Serve Him for Life* 55
6. Conflict—*Agreeing to Disagree* 65
7. Self-Forgetfulness—*Highlight Sibling Accomplishment (Side-Eyeing You, Cain . . .)* 73

#3 AUTHORITY 81

8. Respecting Authority—*Beyond "Because I Said So"* 83
9. Natural Consequences—*Let Him Reap What He Sows* 95
10. Waiting—*Your Call Is Important to Us. Please Continue to Not Whine Like a Two-Year-Old* 102

#4 FUN 109

11. Humor—*A Guy Walks into a Bar . . . Ouch* 111
12. Tedious Responsibilities—*Do the Dishes, Cinderelly* 117

#5 BRAVERY 123

13. Failure—*Practice Makes Perfect Opportunities for Making Mistakes* 125
14. Risk—*Ride the Skateboard! Jump from the High Dive! Try Out for the Team!* 131
15. Grit—*Build an Expensive, Nonfunctioning Rocket* 137

#6 TENDERNESS 145

16. Wonder—*"Wow!" Isn't Just for Owen Wilson* 147
17. Accurate Appraisal of Self—*I'm Talking about the Boy in the Mirror* 155
18. Grace—*Giving and Receiving* 167

#7 CREATIVITY 171

19. Get Outside—*The Best Place for Our Cutest Wrecking Balls* 173
20. Boredom—*"If You're Really That Bored, You Can Fold This Basket of Laundry"* 180

#8 EMOTIONAL DURABILITY 185

21. Language for Feelings—*Beyond Shouting, Stuffing, and Blaming* 187
22. Gratitude—*Thanks a Lot* 197
23. Rest—*Sleep? Isn't There an App for That?* 202

Concluding Thoughts 211
Acknowledgments 213
Notes 215

INTRODUCTION

A person's worldview is primarily formed between 15 months and 13 years of age.[1]

—George Barna, "American Worldview Inventory 2020"

By the age of seven years, a child born today will have spent one full year of [24-hour] days watching screen media.

—Dr. Aric Sigman, "Time for a View on Screen Time"

We are in a battle for the hearts of our kids.

—Molly DeFrank

The nurse wheeled me from my hospital room toward our waiting car. My mind could only think of one thing, the enormity of my new job: mom. I *must* be the best mom to the seven-pound newborn in my arms. The only problem? I'd only been at this job for a day, and I had no clue what I was doing. I glanced at the nurses' station as we rolled past.

"Wait!" I put my feet on the ground, causing the wheelchair to screech to a halt.

"Yes?" the nurse asked.

"What . . . what do I do when I get home?"

"Feed the baby every two and a half to three hours, just like you've been doing. Sleep when you can," she smiled.

"Okay . . ." I lifted my feet back onto the footrests, and Nurse Common Sense began to wheel us along again.

I looked again at the nurses' station—all of them calm, controlled, totally not stressed about caring for a hospital full of screaming babies. They knew so much more than I did! Shouldn't I be required to stay here longer, caring for a brand-new human that I loved more than life? The stakes had never felt higher. And I had never felt less capable of doing a great job.

"Wait!" I engaged my foot brakes again. (Probably knocking myself out of the running for nurse's favorite patient.)

"Yes?" she calmly replied.

"What if something happens? What if I have a question but there's no one to ask?" It seemed almost criminal to release me into the world with this perfect baby. Shouldn't I need a credential or at least some training hours?

The nurse walked to the station and scribbled a phone number on a Post-it note.

"Here," she said, smiling. "We are here 24/7. If you have a question, call the nurses' station."

I clung to that piece of paper like it had the nuclear launch codes.

Six kids and many foster kids later, I've learned about a weird paradox in parenting. The stakes—and parental mistakes—are incredibly high. What are invested parents supposed to do with that reality?

WE are people responsible for forming our kids' hearts, minds, characters, and worldviews. WE are responsible for cultivating the humans we care about most on the planet.

Um.

HELLO? That's kind of a big deal!

That, and . . .

Parents are human people with limited capacities. We can only endure so many sibling spats that resemble scenes from *Dumb and*

Dumber. We can only make so many gourmet dinners that our kids earnestly declare to be "almost as good as Little Caesars!" We pour blood, sweat, and tears into our kids, only to have their five-year-old selves tell the teacher, "I taught *myself* to read." Oh, really? I must have dreamed about those thirty-seven hours of helping you sound out Bob Books while you farted on my lap.

We cannot work under these conditions.

But we must.

MISSION-MINDED BOY MOM

Yes, this gig is hard. But we must roll up our sleeves. Because the world is vying to form the hearts, minds, and worldviews of our kids. Culture diminishes the foundational role of family and parents. From "children's" books espousing X-rated material, to more subtle but insidious lies on TV, social media, and even in schools—today's parents must be vigilant and committed to intentionally forming our kids. And we need to do it every day. This is true for all kids, but for the sake of this book, we're going to specifically cover raising boys. Why?

Our culture is launching an all-out attack on masculinity and the unique importance of boyhood. Raising boys does not always mean baseball and bugs. But just because a few gender stereotypes aren't universal doesn't mean that we reject every difference between males and females. God's design for male and female is a gift. Strong, godly men are the backbone of a flourishing world. Good men provide for, protect, and serve their families in irreplaceable ways. The design for family is beautifully harmonious. Unfortunately, boys today are surrounded by accusations that their very existence is toxic, are told that their biological makeup is a problem and that the future is female. It's time for a mom huddle.

All cultural moments have pressed on various aspects of Christianity, forcing believers to slow down and discern what is true versus what is culturally concocted. Today, many Christian parents

> As Christians and moms, we have a duty to our
> boys. They need us to teach them what is true
> about who they are—and what isn't. They need
> us to help build strong men of godly character.

feel immense pressure to bow to the cultural idea that the differences between boys and girls aren't real. This assertion is false, biologically, biblically, and common-sensically. (If you'll allow my newly invented word.)

What does it mean to raise up boys in this cultural moment? Is a mom's job to serve as our child's genie, maid, and personal chicken-nugget chef? Are we on a mission to grant every whim and wish, or are we working to slough off his sinful tendencies, teach objective truth, and affirm his identity as assigned by a good God?

If we aren't careful, in an effort to be inclusive and loving, we will open our minds so wide that common sense falls out. The erasure of boyhood is harmful both to our sons as individuals and to society as a whole.

As Christians and moms, we have a duty to our boys. They need us to teach them what is true about who they are—and what isn't. They need us to help build strong men of godly character. We can start from square one.

Real masculinity means developing and deploying the skills and courage to protect, provide, and serve others. You'll find examples of this throughout the Bible. Noah worked diligently to build that ark in obedience to God, protecting and providing for his family.[2] Young David courageously and faithfully battled a giant to serve God.[3] We also see a merciful and tender side to David when he spared Saul's life in that cave, driven by a desire to honor God.[4] Boaz generously shared his wealth with widows in his community.[5] Paul developed skills to provide for himself so that he was not a financial burden on society but was economically self-sufficient.[6] There are a lifetime of lessons about masculinity to glean from and emulate in Scripture.

For the sake of space, we'll end with the ultimate, perfect example of masculinity—Jesus, who came not to be served, but to serve.[7]

If you're interested in cultivating your young boys to become strong men, harnessing your unique power as a mom to impact your son, I want to help you with that.

THE POWER OF AN INTENTIONAL MOM

Your young son is one hundred percent interested in his relationship with you. You are his world. But this window of his being completely enamored with you coincides exactly with the years when he exhibits some, um, difficult qualities. Our young boys can be impulsive, wild, messy, loud. Sometimes they don't respond well to instruction. Real talk: Sometimes we get irritated with these little dudes and don't want to hang out with them. Like, "Bro, I love you enough to die for you, but after your two-hour meltdown, I do not want to play Hot Wheels with you."

We want to check out. Sometimes we *need* to check out. But the great paradox is that we are exactly who and what our young boys need during their formative years. Studies have demonstrated that a boy's relationship with his mother is the bedrock for his future relationships, mental health, and well-being.

Mothers are uniquely attuned to their sons—we have the privilege of modeling sacrificial servant leadership to our boys. We lead by example, and through cultivating their capacities for relational tenderness and mental and emotional fortitude. Dads have an irreplaceable impact on their sons, to be sure. But moms are privileged to clock more minutes with our kids.[8] Let's make them count!

After working with educators, parents, and researching trends in today's kids, I've identified eight specific areas for moms to cultivate their boys. Experts have been cranking out evidence showing specific areas of current need. I've condensed those here, in a non-boring way.

These are eight critical needs of growing up that—due to cultural changes—boys aren't getting:

1. *Belonging.* Boys today are increasingly lonely. (Twenty percent of Americans are so lonely that it poses a health risk as significant as smoking a pack of cigarettes per day!)[9] How can mothers cultivate a strong sense of belonging in the hearts of their sons? We will kick off the first three chapters with practical ideas to help your boy understand that he is fully known and fully loved by his family and by God.

2. *Relationship.* Two-thirds of young men surveyed said "no one really knows me."[10] How can you help your son build and maintain relationships? High-quality relationships are the best buffer for mental health and your best tool for spiritual development. Chapters 4–7 will cover this.

3. *Authority.* God tells us to respect Him and to obey His commandments.[11] The world tells our sons to chase their own happiness. How can moms teach their boys to honor authority? In a world where this concept is increasingly rare, chapters 8–10 will provide helpful tools you can use today.

4. *Fun.* Anxiety in boys today is through the roof. Did you know that humor and laughter can diminish the effects of stress and anxiety?[12] Chapters 11 and 12 cover ideas for helping your son have the right kind of fun, and for infusing fun into everyday life.

5. *Bravery.* Kids today are more afraid to take basic risks—but risk-taking is required for growing in confidence and bravery. Chapters 13–15 will help you build your son's sense of courage and confidence to tackle life's challenges.

6. *Tenderness.* We want to raise strong boys with soft hearts. Cultivating a proper sense of tenderness is possible! Chapters 16–18 will explore the how.

7. *Creativity*. Eight-year-olds are spending five and a half hours per day consuming digital entertainment.[13] If your son's creativity is being stifled, you can reawaken creative exploration in the real world. Chapters 19 and 20 will show you how.

8. *Emotional durability*. Teach your son to express himself in a healthy way instead of the cultural norm of numbing out on a device. Chapters 21–23 will show you how to give him language for his emotions, build his sense of gratitude, and provide rest for his body and soul.

We're wise to step back and take note of how our culture is shaping or not shaping our boys. That's why the chapters ahead include research explaining why these components are critical to raising sons generally, and how today's boys are uniquely left wanting in these areas.

You'll find practical and biblical tools for building up our boys by helping them flex their muscles. Best of all, you'll find tools for reinvigorating connection with the humans you love most.

A BEDROCK OF MOTHERLY FAITH

Throughout the chapters ahead, I'll give you specific, practical tools to train up your boys in the faith. But the most important thing we can do to raise boys who understand that their value is in God is to cultivate a robust personal faith of our own.

If you read this book like a checklist, it's going to feel stressful and exhausting. Instead, prioritize your own active faith and Bible reading in community with other believers. Your kids are watching you live that out. Share tidbits of God working in your life with your boys. Rest in His Word. Depend on Him to show up for you as you pray during your hardest moments. Live authentically and honestly in pursuit of Christ.

This book is best read through a lens of faith that God is sovereign, even over the hearts of our sons. Resting in that truth allows us to use the tools and ideas within these pages to both strive for godliness ourselves and to train our boys in godliness—without panic-breathing into a paper bag on the daily.

> **Train yourself to be godly.** For physical training is of some value, but godliness has value for all things, holding promise for both the present life and the life to come. This is a trustworthy saying that deserves full acceptance. **That is why we labor and strive, because we have put our hope in the living God, who is the Savior of all people, and especially of those who believe.**
>
> 1 Timothy 4:7–10, emphasis added

So we do strive to live out this faith we profess. We strive to train up godly young men. And we do it while fully trusting in God's sovereignty.

#1 BELONGING

The world: "Our value and worth depend on our performance and achievement."

Mission-minded boy mom: "We love our kids unconditionally, which reflects the way God loves us unconditionally. I'll teach my son that his value and belonging never waver, even when he blows it."

No matter what happens, your son will always be your baby. A son belongs to his family *forever*. God's design for family is a gift. It is a daily reminder to our kids that they have a place in the world where they are unconditionally known and loved. It's in everyday family life that your son learns that he belongs to a much bigger family—the family of God. Unfortunately, our culture attempts to erode this bedrock of our kids' sense of security and love. We mamas will not allow it. We must teach our young sons that they belong unconditionally. This is the foundation for everything that follows.

We will teach our sons that they always belong in our family, even when they act like knuckleheads. We will show our boys their lives have purpose, given to them by God. And we will impart these beautiful truths in simple, everyday ways, like family dinner.

VALUE

MORE THAN MANY SPARROWS

A child who is not embraced by the village will burn it down to feel its warmth.

—African proverb

Do you think our sons know that we're kind of obsessed with them?

One of my friends cringe-laughed while telling me that she and her husband brought a lengthy list of observations to baby's week-old checkup. "Here, Doctor. We charted every meal and every poop."

"Okay," the doctor said, restraining a smile. "You can keep that."

No one on planet earth loves your son like his mama. Who else would track and discuss the content and frequency of his eliminated substances? Only true love makes you crazy enough to do that. Perhaps you didn't track your own son's diaper contents in a journal, but you are no doubt the world's most trained and knowledgeable

21

expert on him. No one loves that boy like you have from day one. Even when the only noteworthy thing he did was require a diaper change—your love for him was indestructible, indescribable, uncontainable.

Why?

Because a good God designed it that way. God loves people because He is love, not because people are impressive. Babies bring exactly nothing helpful or productive to the table. But moms are wired by God to love and value them beyond measure. (And I hope you take this to heart for yourself too—that God loves you completely on your most productive days, and on your least.) He generously allows us to grasp this truth, and then reflect that sweet parent-child relationship with our own kids.

Sure, our boys might drive us to pop an angry vein in our forehead or throw a grown-up tantrum. But we still love the junk out of those wild creatures. In fact, they drive us to the brink of exhaustion and twitchiness *because* we love them so much! If any other human person did half of the annoying things that one of my children did on a bad day, I would be *out*. But with our kids, we are ride or die. We are here for *life*.

When my little guy ditches kindergarten for the second time in a week to eat stolen candy in the cafeteria. When he leaves his stinky sports socks on the living room floor—again. When he kicks his brother in the shin over a Pokémon-card property dispute . . . I don't love you any less, dude, but I'm mad as heck right now. I'm mad *because* I love you and I want you to not be on the track to delinquency at age five, annoy your future wife, or spend your teen years in juvie.

THE MAIN THING

In the day-to-day stress of carpool, groceries, meal planning, and refereeing sibling spats, we can occasionally miss the forest for the trees. We lose our marbles for cosmically small reasons: another misplaced jacket, a spilled smoothie, finding clumps of toothpaste shellacked to the sink—again. But let's zoom out for a second, because I think our frustrations are truly rooted in a deep care. We want the best for them in the long term. . . . But we don't always give *them* the broader context.

Have you ever had an identity crisis? Let me tell you about one of mine. For whatever reason, I've always enjoyed compliments, head-pats, trophies, awards, metrics, job promotions. You get the idea. My value was placed in measurable accomplishment. After working in a high-stress job for several years, I quit my job to stay home and raise babies. I was promptly punched in the face by an identity crisis. My inner critic was brutal. "So, you don't earn any money now?" "Why isn't your house sparkling clean if you're home?" "Why aren't you more fit?" "Wow, it only takes two little babies to show you how incompetent you are."

That chick can suck a lemon, btw. In case she lives in your head too.

It has taken me *years* to come to terms with the truth that my value is not in any sort of performance metric or accolade. My value lies in the fact that I am a human being created by a good God. I have innate dignity and worth because I'm created in God's image. Value that is rooted in an eternal God cannot be changed. Phew!

Moms have the privilege of teaching this foundation of inherent, unchanging value to our boys when they are small. We have the opportunity to lay this unshakable foundation. We have the opportunity to prevent or buffer our son's own future identity crises. When he doesn't make the team, when his top college rejects him, or when the crush doesn't like him back. (Which would obviously mean she is blind and crazy.)

A mom has the enormous privilege of communicating to her son that his value does not depend on: how clean his room is, how many times he was disciplined this week, whether he forgot his jacket on the bus (again), or left his bike out in the rain. Even if each of these instances makes your eye twitch, they don't change your son's value.

(Neither does our angry eye twitch change our own inherent value, praise the Lord.)

We possess a deep, unchanging love for our little dude. We are also divinely appointed to be his primary authority figure for these formative years. Our love and authority make us uniquely credible to teach him early and often that he is valuable because he is a human being made in the image of God. This understanding guards against future uncertainties. *What if I'm not the best on the team? What if I sit the bench the whole season? What if I never get past this speech impediment? What if I can't understand my math homework? What if I keep blowing it?*

Our divinely appointed authority and loving influence make us perfectly positioned to teach our boys how to swap out their internal "what if" script, and instead say, "Even if I don't make the team . . . Even if I sit the bench all season . . . Even if I blow it . . . I am valuable and loved, and that will never, ever change. Because I'm made by God who gives me value." (Take a minute to remind yourself this truth about your own value: *Even if* you snapped at a carful of kids this morning . . . *Even if* you can't get a handle on the laundry . . . you are valuable and loved, and that will never change.)

HOW EARLY CAN I START TEACHING MY LITTLE BOY ABOUT HIS VALUE?

John Newton (former slave trader, epic conversion story, dude who wrote a little ditty you may have heard of called "Amazing Grace") credits his mama with the formation of his faith. "She made it the chief business and pleasure of her life to instruct me, and bring me up in the nurture and admonition of the Lord."[1]

Newton spent a good chunk of his life wandering from truth, entangled in worldly pursuits. He eventually returned to the faith his mother instilled, and had this to say about it:

> Though in process of time I sinned away all the advantages of these early impressions, yet they were for a great while a restraint upon me;

they returned again and again, and it was very long before I could wholly shake them off; and when the Lord at length opened my eyes, I found a great benefit from the recollection of them.[2]

Newton's mom taught, formed, molded him, affecting his worldview and faith deeply.

You guys, Newton was six when his mother died of tuberculosis. *Six.*

The eternity-altering impact that John's mother imprinted on her son happened before most children learn to read.

Friends, this is incredible news for us normies. Sometimes we hear about the historical greats, assuming they were part angel or made of different stuff than you and me. No, ma'am. I'd bet the change in my pocket that lady Elizabeth wanted to tear off her bonnet on occasion. "John, if you rip a hole in another pair of breeches, I will put your rocking horse out to pasture."

I have exactly no evidential basis for the pretend quote I just wrote for our girl Lizzy, but I do know that the best women and mothers are made of *exactly the same stuff* as you and me, okay? Great moms have good days, and bad days. Great moms make eternal deposits into the lives and hearts of their boys, trusting that God uses all of us to plant seeds that will grow into valiant oaks one day. Great moms fall down, get back up, and do better next time. Most of all, great moms look for opportunities to impart truth to their littlest ones.

If Newton's weak and sickly mother was able to instill the kind of heart-shaping experiences and foundational truths in her son when he was teensy, certainly we can too. Within a few years, John would reject his mother's teachings outwardly. But inside, the truth she sowed would eventually anchor him. Those little sprouts

Great moms make eternal deposits into the lives and hearts of their boys, trusting that God uses all of us to plant seeds that will grow into valiant oaks one day.

tapped his shoulder for years, beckoning him back to the life he would embrace.

Every time we tell our boy where his value comes from, we plant a seed.

MOTHERING THROUGH EVERYDAY MESSES WITH GRACE *IS* CONVEYING VALUE

When one of my sons was two, he was *very* challenging behaviorally. He was a sensory-seeking, wild little man. One morning during breakfast, I took a phone call from the doctor's office in our family room, adjacent to the kitchen. *He'll be okay in his high chair,* I thought. *It'll take him five minutes to get through his pile of waffles. I'll take the call real quick. It'll be fine.*

That's when the narrator would say, "It would not, in fact, be fine."

During this four-minute phone call, the child climbed out of his high chair and onto the kitchen table. He found our Costco-sized bottle of maple syrup and poured himself a generous, sticky puddle. Then he sat in it, glugging more syrup onto the table.

I surveyed the damage, flabbergasted, overwhelmed, and annoyed as heck. I could not believe the situation: I'd left the room to talk to a doctor, who wanted to address my concerns *about my son's sensory-seeking behaviors.* The scene deserved a verse in Alanis Morissette's song "Ironic," don't you think?

I'm smiling while typing that, because this kid is now an honor-roll student, a great athlete, recently baptized, thoughtful, and kind. He understands the gospel. He understands the calling on his life. He is also a teenager. That sticky scene is far in the rearview.

And I assure you, if some mom of a teenage boy had come to tell me that I needed to teach my mini frat boy about his God-given value back then, I'd have stared like she had three heads and tossed her a rag to help me wipe up syrup.

Here's the encouragement to you, mom of mini frat brothers. The physical labor you pour into your tiny sons, day in, day out—it *is* teaching him that he is valued. When I took a deep breath, wiped the syrup, bathed the sticky boy, told him I loved him, hugged him, and put him down for a nap . . . that reflected the love of our good Father.

Your everyday physical acts of care and love for your little dude show him he is valued. And the years of selflessly caring for him are earning you the credibility to explain the value of the life God gave him, as he grows old enough to understand.

HOW TO INTENTIONALLY TEACH OUR SONS ABOUT THEIR INHERENT VALUE

Beyond your everyday love and care for your son, here are specific ways to help him understand his value as a child of God.

Pray with your boy from day one. Pray over him before he can talk. Show him at bedtime and mealtimes, we bow our heads and pray. For a long time, he will have no idea what is happening. But he will notice and wonder, *Mom and Dad do this thing before we eat. Why? Who are we talking to? Must be important if it's every time. I saw Mom buy these groceries at Walmart. Who is she thanking?*

What does prayer have to do with teaching value? We are demonstrating for our kids that the biggest heroes in their life—mom and dad—submit to something much, much bigger than themselves. Who is this God they submit to? What does that God have to say about him? He is the One who gives us value.

Teach your boy from day one the story of creation, the fall, and redemption. God made people. God loves people. People sinned. God loves us so much that He made a rescue plan so we could have a way back to Him, even though people keep choosing yucky sin instead of our good God. He sent Jesus to pay the consequence for our sins, even though Jesus never sinned. All we have to do is believe in Him and we are rescued! He didn't save us because we have achieved all the things. In fact, He made His rescue plan *before* we were born and sinned all our sins! Why? Because God finds every human life unspeakably valuable.

A couple of resources: *The Jesus Storybook Bible* by Sally Lloyd-Jones and the ESV Study Bible.

Sing hymns, worship songs, classic kids' songs that instill truth. Examples: "Amazing Grace," "Good, Good Father" by Chris Tomlin, "Genesis, 1:1–27 (KJV)" by King Things, "Who You Say I Am" by Hillsong Worship.

Talk to your son about how deeply loved and cherished he is. If you're anything like me, you really have to be on the lookout for these opportunities. We are busy, so use the car rides. Use the good-night kiss. Use the pre-nap hug or the postgame encouragement to tell your boy: "I enjoy you so much. I am so glad you are mine. What a privilege it is to watch you grow. What a gift to be your mom." The correction and direction exchanges we have with our boys are going to happen no matter what. But the intentional encouragement and connection convos are the ones we need to work to make happen.

Conversation starters to remind your son of his inherent, un-earned, unshakable value

- Recount your son's birth or adoption story. Be sure to include how you felt: excited, nervous, brimming with anticipation. Tell him how much you loved him before you even met him.
- Tell him how you came up with his name.
- Share funny stories of your worrying too much, or asking the doctor silly questions because you cared so much about protecting him.
- Share cute sayings from his toddler self and adorable baby stories; open the scrapbooks, pull out the keepsakes. Watch home videos of him as a baby.
- When appropriate, invite his input on family decisions—taking his ideas seriously. One simple way to do this is in meal planning. "Any ideas for dinners or desserts this week? What are your favorites?"

PURPOSE

PARENTS, THE ORIGINAL STRENGTHSFINDER

God created us male and female in His own image to glorify Him.

—New City Catechism

She said it was good enough to be in a book. Nothing anyone has said to me since has made me feel any happier.

—Stephen King, recounting his mom's compliment of his writing at age six, *On Writing*[1]

There are two different ways I see Christian parents missing opportunities to teach our sons their true purpose of loving God and loving people.

First, we're buying into the cultural lie that the purpose of life is to chase personal happiness. The world tells our sons that the purpose of their lives is to make themselves happy. Well-intentioned parents (even within the church!) have bought into this idea, catering to their kids' whims, only to regret it when their twenty-three-year-old son is still financially dependent on dad and mom, purposeless, unmotivated, living in the basement playing video games. We must correct the false narrative that the purpose of life is happiness. If we don't, our sons will experience crushing blows anytime they don't feel happy. The idea that life's purpose is to chase our own feelings sounds a lot like the lie Eve believed in the garden all those years ago. Unquestioningly following our feelings isn't freedom, it's self-imprisonment. How constraining to believe that if you aren't happy, you're not living your life on purpose.

The second way parents are missing it when it comes to teaching our boys their true purpose: We take a good goal and crown it as our highest priority—our driving purpose. (Straight A's, athletic scholarship, first place in underwater basket-weaving championships.) Just this week I attended a sports event where I watched a teenage boy become utterly undone by a loss. This student loudly disrespected the opposing team's coach and had embarrassingly poor sportsmanship. I glanced at his mom, waiting for some type of correction. Instead, she defended her son's behavior. "Please don't talk to him, he is upset right now," she huffed at the people around her. Christian parents must instill a deeper purpose in our kids. If honoring God is his driving purpose, then your son will not become undone when he loses a junior high game that will be forgotten in a few days. (Even if he does fall apart after a loss—which we all do at times—you will be able to coach him back into the comforting foundational truths about his purpose you have instilled over the years.)

If we aren't intentional, we will miss the mark when it comes to anchoring our sons in their true purpose. The data shows that purposelessness in a generation of boys has already become its own epidemic. While life expectancy for women has remained static, male life expectancy has declined. At least 90 percent of mass shooters and prisoners are male.[2] Women are more likely than men to graduate high school and finish college.[3] We shouldn't expect any different, as we've watched the historical, biblical, and biological understandings of male and female ripped apart, without any sane plan for how to reconstruct those ideas. "The future is female." "Masculinity is toxic." "Fight the patriarchy." Culture spews these mantras at our boys. Manhood has been pummeled, without any appreciation for the admirable and important aspects of masculinity that our world depends on. Our society needs strong, steady protectors and providers willing to work the most dangerous and physically demanding jobs. In a culture where traditional ideas of masculinity are rejected, boys are understandably growing confused and hopeless. But not your son, not under your watch. Your boy is created in the image of God, with unique interests and giftings. Your son has an important purpose in this world. To use his voice, talents, strength, and his masculinity to love God, and love people. Instilling a biblical worldview from his youngest days is the antidote to purposelessness.

TEACHING GODLY PURPOSE TO TINY, WILY HOOLIGANS

If you are reading this while watching your toddler son lick cat food off the floor—I realize these ideas may sound lofty. Stick with me, because they are true for every human who has ever lived on earth, and they're true for your little floor-licker too. (Half my kids were floor-lickers. For all we know, Moses himself was a floor-licker. They grow out of it. Promise.)

Thankfully, moms are perfectly positioned to instill a firm foundation of purpose in the hearts and minds of our sons.

Here's where it gets fun. As mom, you are ideally situated to observe your son, and identify his God-given strengths. You get to zoom in and cultivate those, and even help him understand

Moms are perfectly positioned to instill a firm foundation of purpose in the hearts and minds of our sons.

how he can use those gifts for kingdom purposes. You also get to sit with him and process life when his soccer-pro dreams don't align with his two-left-feet reality. You get to reassure him that God works all things for the good of those who love Him, and who have been called according to His purpose (Romans 8:28). The broken Lego tower, the bad day at school, moving to a new city. For people who love God, He will use the junkiest parts of our lives *for good.*

Now let's get specific.

IDENTIFYING AND CULTIVATING YOUR SON'S UNIQUE GIFTS FOR KINGDOM PURPOSES

If your boy is athletic, or brilliant in math, or particularly adept at Lego towers, you can already imagine where God may use his talents in the future: on a sports team, as an engineer, or as an architect.

But what about the less obvious stuff? I'm talking about the character stuff. The stuff you find when you look under the rock and see all the squirmy bugs. You may find impatience, laziness, aggression, selfishness. Can we pause for a second and just say, welcome to the club! There is no such thing as a kid without flaws; but sometimes there are parents in denial. If you can identify your son's areas for growth potential, good job! You're already ahead of the game.

What if I told you that your son's most annoying trait might just become his best asset?[4]

Let us don our rose-colored glasses for a moment, shall we? Does your son's incessant movement put the Energizer Bunny to shame? Cheers to endurance and stamina! Your boy can't drop an argument? Persistence properly channeled will serve him well in a court of law.

As his mom, *you* are the person who knows your son's strengths and weaknesses best. You can see the aspects of his nature and temperament that will help him, and those that will hinder him. Sometimes input from teachers and Sunday school volunteers will help provide insight.

Here are a few seemingly difficult personality traits you may notice in your boys—and ideas for how to help shape and cultivate them for kingdom purposes. I've included a few references to biblical men who exhibited these traits but eventually overcame them or used those traits for good. Use a children's Bible to tell your boys the stories of these flawed but faithful men who loved God. Look how they served God, and how He used these men to bring about His good purposes.

Negative trait	Same trait as a positive
Stubborn	Firm in convictions
Biblical dude who exemplified	
Moses—initially balked when God called him to lead the Israelites. But he finally went. God grew him in fortitude, and he stood up to Pharoah and even led two million Israelites out of Egypt.	
How moms can help	
Look for ways to affirm your son making good use of his strong convictions, and praise that at dinner. Share it with your husband when your son can overhear. When your son cedes a point, tell him how mature that is, and that some adults are still learning how to do this. Team sports provide plenty of opportunities for stubborn kids to practice compromise. Let him navigate his own way through conflicts (assuming no one is getting hurt). It's okay if he blows it. That will make for a great learning conversation on the ride home.	

Negative trait	Same trait as a positive
Regulator/Meddler	Clear view of justice
Biblical dude who exemplified	
Paul—was a devoted Jewish leader who persecuted Christians. After God changed Paul's heart, he redirected that keen sense of right and wrong, putting it to work for God and His kingdom.	

How moms can help

Affirm that he has a strong, clear view of right and wrong. Help him parse out when it's his job to speak into a situation, and when it's not. Siblings or classmates arguing adjacent to him? When should he intervene? Explain to him future careers in which a clear understanding of right and wrong is very helpful for society: police officers, judges, attorneys, writers, pastors. We need these people to help society function. But we also need them to know when and where to apply the law. My favorite proverb to share with kids who meddle in sibling fights: "Don't be quick to get mixed up in someone else's fight. That's like grabbing a stray dog by its ears" (Proverbs 26:17 NIrV). Yikes. An effective visual. You can share the proverb and ask a few questions. "Is it a good or bad idea to go up to an angry stray dog and surprise it by grabbing it by the ears? Why? Solomon, the wisest man who ever lived, compares grabbing a stray dog to what? Why do you think he compares those two actions? What can happen if you get involved in a fight that isn't yours? Can you think of a time when you got involved in someone else's fight? How did that go?"

Negative trait	Same trait as a positive
Fearless	Brave

Biblical dude who exemplified

David—Tiny, preteen, shepherd boy David voluntarily fought eleven-foot Goliath, who had been taunting and terrifying Israel's army. Goliath's *armor* weighed 125 pounds. No man in Israel's army would dare fight Goliath. Young David demonstrated faith and courage when he proclaimed, "The LORD does not deliver by sword or by spear; for the battle is the LORD's and He will give you into our hands" (1 Samuel 17:47 NASB). David ran toward this giant, and aimed his slingshot at him—pow, right in the kisser—giant down. When fearlessness meets faith, incredible things happen.

How moms can help

I see no mention of David's mom in the story, but I can only imagine her response to his idea. "You want to take your slingshot to the ogre on the front lines and do *what*!?" Fearless little boys have turned many mothers' hair gray. But take heart! That fearless spirit can be wielded for great things, in time. Share the story of David and Goliath with your boy, pointing to the winning combo of courage and faith. Ask him, "Did David run full speed immediately when he saw the giant? What did he do beforehand? Did he take on this fight for himself? Who did David want to be glorified or celebrated after his win?" Fearlessness in the flesh makes for plenty of stupid life choices. But courage in faith creates heroes."

Negative trait	Same trait as a positive
Overly chatty	Engaged conversationalist

Biblical dude who exemplified

Joseph—(robe braggadocio)—"Hey, brothers. Had the weirdest dream last night—that I was your master! Crazy, right? Wow, look how cool my robe is that Dad gave me. . . . Oh, you guys didn't get one? Weird." I want to think I'd be the levelheaded sibling, but dang if I wouldn't want to vote Joseph off the island too. Not sell him, but like, send him away for a little while. Joseph's brothers sold him into slavery. But later, Joseph's wise words and counsel would earn him favor with the pharaoh, and that eventually all worked out . . . ish.

How moms can help

Kindly remind your son that loving his neighbor means that his words should bless—not burden—their ears. Thinking before speaking helps everyone. "Too much talk leads to sin. Be sensible and keep your mouth shut" (Proverbs 10:19 NLT). Help him to remember the Golden Rule, and to ask himself if his words pass the Golden Rule test before he lets them out of his mouth. There's a reason we have two ears but only one tongue. And notice that our one tongue sits behind two lips and many teeth!

Negative trait	Same trait as a positive
Impulsive	Emotionally aware

Biblical dude who exemplified

Peter—led with his emotions at times. When Jesus told Peter that He would face death on the cross, Peter's response was, "Never, Lord! This shall never happen to you!" Jesus replied, "Get behind me, Satan! You are a stumbling block to me; you do not have in mind the concerns of God, but merely human concerns."[5] Yikes. I wouldn't have liked to be on the receiving end of that rebuke.

But Peter's zeal also led him to worship and to his beautiful pursuit of Jesus. After Jesus's resurrection, He appeared to the disciples from the shore as they were out in their fishing boat, still a hundred yards away. When John realized the man they saw was Jesus, he exclaimed, "It is the Lord!" Peter immediately jumped out of the boat and swam to shore. (A hundred yards!) The rest of the disciples followed . . . in the boat.[6] There is something very endearing about that kind of passion.

> **How moms can help**
>
> This is going to be a long-term, long-game commitment, my friend. Our most emotional dudes will need years of practice to understand how to navigate their big feelings. Remind your son that emotions are meant to be felt, but not to drive the ship all the time. Help show him that sometimes we need to physically move our bodies to process our emotions. Sometimes we need to remove ourselves to a private room to cry. Sometimes we need to cry to a trusted person. I've watched one of my emotional boys mature beautifully in this area over the years. His emotions are a gift, as he has learned the whens and hows of processing and sharing. More on helping our sons navigate emotional processing in chapters 21–23.

YOUR SON IS CALLED TO A UNIVERSAL *AND* UNIQUE PURPOSE— EVEN WHEN YOU CAN'T SEE IT

Here is the truth I hope sticks with you as you wrap up this chapter. There is so much we do not know—yet. I wonder if God will give us a slideshow of solved mysteries someday in heaven. What a thrill it would be to watch the ways He used our hardest trials for good. What an honor it would be to observe the intricate way God wove your son's setbacks and your biggest prayers into triumphant purpose.

I may not know how your plans for your son have been frustrated. Maybe he didn't make the team. Maybe he can't pronounce that dang letter, therapy be darned. Maybe he inexplicably mimed to his teacher that he was struck with temporary muteness. (I wish that last one wasn't drawn from my own parenting experience, but alas.)

Here is what I do know. God has called your son for a purpose. He wants all people to be reconciled to himself through Jesus. And He made your boy with unique gifts, traits, and interests. God uses all things for good, even when we can't see it yet, and even if the stress in the meantime gives us moms a splitting headache. We cannot know how God is currently working out the setbacks and muck for His good purposes. But we know that He is doing just that, even in the smallest details of your boy's life.

Today we can choose to trust Him as we wait to find out what He will reveal to us in time. We can also choose to teach and shape our sons, reminding them of their purpose in Christ, and the call on their lives to use everything they have to love God and love people. There is no one on the planet better positioned to bang this drum for your son, reminding him day in and day out: You have a purpose designed by God; I can't wait to see how He uses your life for good.

FAMILY DINNER

CHAOTIC, DELICIOUS, LIFE-CHANGING

I'm a family therapist . . . I could be out of business if more families had regular family dinners, because so many of the things that I try to do in family therapy actually get accomplished by regular dinners.

—Anne Fishel, in Harvard School of Education interview[1]

Every known human society rests firmly on the learned nurturing behavior of men. . . .

This behavior, being learned, is fragile and can disappear rather easily under social conditions that no longer teach it effectively.

—Margaret Mead, *Male and Female*

"I lived in many foster homes growing up, but one home changed my life," a speaker shared at a foster parent commencement in Southern California. "This one foster family—they ate dinner together at night.

And they went around the table sharing the highs and lows from the day. Everyone had a chance to share and talk. . . . They were a normal family. Kids in the family still fought. But afterwards, they'd make up and hug it out. This family was different. My siblings and I only stayed in their home for two weeks, but I'll never forget those family dinners."

My brother, also a foster/adoptive parent, shared that encouraging story with me. With my six kids around the dinner table, plenty of nights look more like *Lord of the Flies* than a Hallmark commercial. When you're living and working in the trenches, it's easy to assume that just because you can't *see* the impact you're having on your kids, you're not *making* an impact on your kids. This misperception isn't new to you and me. The visible chaos of mom life leads to infinite moments of frustration. That's when it's most important for us to remember Paul's exhortation to "fix our eyes not on what is seen, but on what is unseen, since what is seen is temporary, but what is unseen is eternal" (2 Corinthians 4:18).

We don't get to see the tangled strings in our son's heart becoming untangled while he verbally dumps a day's worth of kindergarten stress over spaghetti. We don't get to see the neural pathways light up when he finally plops into his regular dinner seat and exhales, knowing that he's sitting around a table where he is fully known, and fully loved. We can't know the generational impact on a young boy whose exhausted mama prays over the meal she made, draws out his heart through simple conversation, and teaches him Bible truth.

RESEARCH SAYS FAMILY MEALS PREVENT COUNTLESS PROBLEMS FOR OUR BOYS

It turns out the oft-touted benefits of regular family dinner are supported by decades of research and dozens of studies. Research shows that eating together as a family can lower depression, anxiety, substance-abuse rates, and tobacco use. The simple practice of family dinners can create more resilient kids with higher self-esteem.[2]

Simply enjoying a meal as a family impacts the mind, body, spirit, and academics in powerful and measurable ways. Despite the research, 60 percent of families still do not utilize this tool that's simple, enjoyable, and delicious (depending on who's cooking).

I can't answer for all 60 percent of those respondents. But I do know that when you are parenting little people who are still learning how to be a human—and are not at all fluent in table manners—sit-down dinners can make parents . . . irritable . . . crazy . . . dream of being elsewhere, including but not limited to getting a root canal.

There, I said it.

When we had four kids under six, I remember sitting around the dinner table. On an average night, I'd be in and out of my seat seventeen times. One kid answered nature's urgent and untimely call. Just as I tried to take my first bite of dinner, the child beckoned for help wiping. Another cried because two of the foods on her plate were touching. A different kid stewed over being served the wrong color plate. My husband, David, and I constantly doled out reminders: "Do not talk with your mouth full of food." "Dinner time is not a contact sport. Please wait to tackle your brother until after the meal." I remember staring at David over the noisy, messy table, my eyes saying, "This is hard. I am tired."

Sometimes it's easier to set the kids up with plates and clock out, scrolling away on our devices. Or plop them in front of the TV so we can finally veg. If we aren't careful, we will passively hand over our best opportunities to connect with our kids. God's earliest parenting instruction exhorts moms and dads to teach their kids about God in these very moments. "These commandments that I give you today are to be on your hearts. Impress them on your children. Talk about them when **you sit at home** and when you walk along the road, when you lie down and when you get up" (Deuteronomy 6:6–7, emphasis my own). Don't waste these powerful opportunities to influence and form the heart of your son. Push through the hard moments, fight for them. Don't willingly hand over these golden opportunities to a random online influencer.

> Your family is your son's first experience with social belonging. Family mealtimes reinforce that he belongs, this is his home, these are his people.

Your family is your son's first experience with social belonging. Family mealtimes reinforce that he belongs, this is his home, these are his people. No matter how hard or busy the days are, he will always have this table where he can exhale, be known, and hopefully share some giggles.

On the other end of what felt like two thousand chaotic dinners, we have kids who know how to set the table, eat the food served to them, and do the dishes. (And no one requires mid-meal wiping assistance!) More important, these kids feel that they belong to a family where they are known, loved, held accountable, and celebrated. Moms are privileged to serve as the people who listen to our kids unpack the mental load, bear that load with them, and then provide counsel and context that aligns with our faith. What a massive opportunity to form the hearts and minds of our boys, all while they enjoy the comfort and peace of belonging. Hard to think of a job more important than that. How fun that we get to do this work over delicious food that we have lovingly prepared or purchased.

PRACTICAL WAYS TO MAKE FAMILY MEALS DOABLE

Maybe work, sports, or other commitments make family dinners feel impossible. Don't stress. It doesn't need to be gourmet. You literally just need your people and something to eat. Opportunities abound to sit with your boys over food. Here are a few ideas.

Breakfast before school. Maybe you're a homemade egg-strata kind of girl, or maybe you're a microwaved frozen-egg-burrito lady. Doesn't matter! Grab what is doable for you. One morning in early motherhood, I ran out of bread. My kids loved toast in the morning.

I found an old bag of hamburger buns in the freezer. It was all we had. "Circle toast for breakfast, woohoo!" I slathered those puppies with pb&j. After that, the kids constantly asked me for circle toast. Point is, it doesn't matter what you serve. Peanut butter and banana on toast, served on a napkin. Easy. What matters is that you're creating a space to hang out and eat. If your mornings are crazy hectic, maybe family breakfast won't be your thing. That's okay!

Afternoon snack. Grab a blanket and a box of popsicles. Or a bag of popcorn. Or both! Spread it out on the lawn and snack to your heart's desire. Lie back and identify cloud formations. Tell jokes from the popsicle sticks. If the weather is being sassy, put some cheese and crackers out on the kitchen table. Sometimes when I'm feeling wild, I'll let my kids drink hot chocolate after school and really blow their minds. Pull out a muffin tin and fill each slot with a different snack item, whatever you have in the fridge. If some foods are new to your kids, ask them to rate it, one to ten. Or you can play "Open your mouth and close your eyes, and I'll give you a big surprise," like my mom used to do. I don't recommend being on the receiving end of the surprise if your boys are wily like mine. But it's fun to play this game if your boys are willing. Be sure to keep the snacks enjoyable.

Easy dinners. Family dinner doesn't have to be gourmet or complicated. Pick up a Costco pizza. Gluten- and dairy-free? Grab a rotisserie chicken and a bag of salad on your way home from work or practice. We are in a season of terribly busy afternoons. I have found that if dinner isn't fully prepped by 2:30 p.m., I won't have an opportunity to make it. So I use my Crock-Pot often. Soup can simmer on the stove for a while, if you need to prep dinner during nap time. When I had two kids under two, a mom of four dropped a meal off for our family. I looked at her in awe and asked, "How do you do it?" "You'll figure it out," she smiled. "You'll find little hacks along the way. Put a pot of water on the stove during nap time so you can make spaghetti later. One less step for the evening. You can do this." She was right.

Maybe you need to eat dinner at the baseball field one night. Snack-bar hot dogs in lawn chairs? Awesome! You could also pack some chicken wraps in tortillas and foil. There are endless options. Double-batch soup or a casserole and freeze the second batch. Dinner will be ready very quickly without prep. These are all ideas to take the fuss out of the prep, and help you to not feel stressed, so you can enjoy the mealtime.

SHOWING YOUR BOYS THAT THEY CAN SERVE THE FAMILY TOO

Meal prep is a perfect time to teach your boys about responsibility and sharing the load. As soon as your little dude can walk, he can help. He can put his napkin in the trash. We moved our dishes into a lower cupboard when our kids were small so they could help empty the dishwasher. It turns out that our tiniest boys enjoy helping with tasks because they feel useful. Look for ways your boys can help around the kitchen: set the table, take out the trash, fill the dishwasher. You'll also train them up to be wonderful husbands someday.

The everyday chores associated with mealtime show your sons that they belong in the family. They belong to you, and you to them. You are your own special unit that God chose and made. And you work together because you love each other. Will it get messy? Oh, girl. Messy is the name of the game. But the mess is worth it 1,000 percent.

Family dinners form a shared understanding of belonging. First in your immediate family, and eventually, we pray, in a much bigger family—the family of God. This understanding of belonging is built over simple meals, lovingly assembled or ordered by a good mama. Remember the words of Paul, and of that former foster child. Each time you bring your boys around the table, you're building their sense of belonging—whether you can see it or not.

The world: "My son will be a future pro athlete. The most important thing in his life is his private hitting/pitching/training lessons."

Mission-minded boy mom: "No matter my son's future path, relationships are the bedrock of every success, both on earth and in eternity. Helping him grow in his relationship with God and the people around him is of utmost importance."

Did you know that quality relationships can predict future health, happiness, and longevity?[1] It's true. More than social class, IQ, income, genes, cholesterol levels—quality *relationships* will impact your boy's future.[2] Your son's ability to connect with other humans and negotiate friendships will have massive, lasting implications for the rest of his life. As mom, you get to expand your son's capacity for building relationships. What a huge job! The good news is that you can start today, and the tools are simple. The next four chapters will show you how.

EYE CONTACT

PEEP THE WINDOW TO THE SOUL

I am sending you to them to open their eyes and turn them from darkness to light.

—Acts 26:17–18

Parents of Gen Z kids are like:

"Hurry up and get in the car, Aiden!"

"Put your shoes on, Blayden!"

"Harveigh! Finish your gluten-free matcha acai avocado bonanza bowl. Organic karate is starting in ten minutes!"

Rushin' is the parenting language of our day, amirite?

I had a breakthrough mom moment at the bus stop five years ago. After a full morning of barking orders at my kids to get their shoes/backpack/in the car, etc., the bus rolled up. The kids walked away from me, toward it.

My gears shifted from "Get 'er done" to "Don't leave, precious babies!"

A few days later, on an unrushed morning, I remember sipping coffee, looking into my second-grade son's eyes while he told me about a game he was really into. We had nowhere to be. Instead of waiting for a pause in his description so I could move us along to the next thing, I just listened.

I looked in his eyes while he gushed about his new favorite thing. They lit up in ways that I hadn't been taking the time to notice. It was like a punch in the face to my mom psyche. Well, maybe more like a clarifying slap—a good one. "Do this more," I told myself. "This is the good stuff."

On a bad day, too many of our parent-child interactions consist of mom or dad barking directions and corrections. While these interactions are necessary, the magic of parenting happens in the connection zone, when our interactions are not transactional but relational.

The starting point to this connection is eye contact.

Sound too simple to matter much?

It matters.

MODERN RESEARCH SHOWS US THAT EYE CONTACT GROWS RELATIONSHIPS DEEPER, AND FASTER

Psychologists discovered that relational closeness can be accelerated. One study took groups of strangers, two at a time, and paired them randomly, telling them to ask each other thirty-six questions, then stare into each other's eyes for four minutes.[1] Six months later, one of those randomly paired sets of strangers got married.[2]

In short: Our actions, specifically increasing eye contact, significantly influence relational closeness.

We will get to the conversational piece of this experiment in the next chapter. But let's talk about the power of human eye contact. Looking into another person's eyes opens a gate to their heart. Eye contact ignites connection.

> ## When we seize the power of eye contact—without asking for anything—we are showing our kids that they are fully known by steady, loving grown-ups who are not going anywhere.

After the psychologists' study, another woman attempted her own experiment with a colleague, using the questions from the original research along with the eye contact. Soon after, she and her colleague/study participant were married. She wrote an essay about it for the *New York Times*. Here's how she explained the magic of staring into another person's eyes: "The real crux of the moment was not just that I was really seeing someone, but that I was seeing someone really seeing me."[3]

This is the gold nugget for parents. From birth, our cute little narcissists—I mean babies—are constantly seeking attention, wanting to be looked at, watched, admired.

When we seize the power of eye contact—without asking for anything—we are showing our kids that they are fully known by steady, loving grown-ups who are not going anywhere. Parental love does not change.

Our kids can glimpse this powerful truth (even if they don't quite understand that's what they're seeing) simply through mutual eye contact.

THE COST OF NOT ENOUGH EYE CONTACT

"Kids in foster care have missed out on early childhood bonding experiences with a parent," said the social worker teaching our foster parent licensing class. "Try to replicate these critical but missing components of early childhood. One example? Eye contact. Kids need lots of eye contact from trusted adults. While a child in a loving home may have enjoyed hours of eye contact with their mom while nursing or bottle-feeding, this is often not the case for neglected and abused kids."

My husband and I became foster parents in 2018. This eye-contact training session was seared into my brain. The idea that kids from traumatic backgrounds didn't get enough eye contact, that it compounded their trauma, and that loving adults can help them heal from it . . . It was sad, but empowering and hope-building.

While most parents understand there is value in looking into our baby's eyes as they nurse or bottle-feed, I don't think we appreciate the harm done to children who don't get enough eye contact with parents. Deficits in parent-child eye contact can even lead to brain disorders and psychological problems.[4]

Wait. For real? Yes. Lack of sufficient parent-child eye contact can damage kids' brains and mental health!

Yet here we are, a generation of parents willingly exchanging parent-child interaction for passive entertainment consumption. Kids have swapped the influence of loving, real-life parents for online, unknown "influencers." More time on digital entertainment means less time invested in serve-and-return interactions that are critical to brain architecture.

The most basic form of this back-and-forth interaction is eye contact.

This simple connection activates the brain's reward system, and research also shows that eye contact is critical to building human capacity for empathy.[5]

Some experts even think that the long-touted benefits of breast-feeding babies have more to do with the face-to-face time a mother spends with her baby than with the biochemical compounds in milk![6]

One pediatric epidemiologist and author of a landmark study of breastfeeding moms said, "There are no good data showing that the omega-3 fatty acids in breast milk lead to higher IQs. The bottom line is, we don't know if it's the greater time spent, the social interaction, or the physical contact."[7]

Let's harness this simple, powerful tool. You can give your son the transformative kind of eye contact he needs—right now. Seize the in-between moments of your hectic days: waiting in the parking lot to pick up a sibling, doctor's visits, mealtimes. Opportunities abound. We just need to be intentional about it.

We rationalize that because of our insane schedules, the kids need the time to decompress. So we leave them to their own devices. Literally. Tweens today are staring at their little dopamine-release machines for EIGHT HOURS A DAY, according to Common Sense Media.[8] This is eight hours per day—a full-time job—of pure digital entertainment. Our kids need a better visual anchor. They need to look at something that can look back at them with attention, unconditional love, and guidance. Our kids need—and aren't getting enough—face-to-face connective interaction with their parents.

PLANT GOOD SEEDS

These relational spaces are the vast and fertile relationship fields where we plant every type of seed that will bear fruit in its time. After a drawn-out sibling spat, I will sometimes ask my kids, "What seeds are you planting in your sibling garden? Are you planting kindness and friendship? Forgiveness and grace? Are you watering the seeds? Are you plucking the weeds? Or are you just scattering junk, neglecting the whole lot? With time and tending, beautiful things can grow. But it's going to take work. When you're grown-ups, you'll enjoy the harvest of your diligent relationship tending. But if you neglect instead of tend, the garden won't be much of a garden. Instead, you'll look at each other and say, "I gave you my worst, and you gave me yours. This ain't a vineyard—it's a junkyard."

Let's apply that to parenting.

What are we planting, watering, and cultivating in our sons? Are we staking the little sprouts before they're ready to stand on their own? Plenty of external struggles outside our control are certain to pop up. But as far as it depends on us, we must pour in, planting seeds of virtue. We must train up, pluck weeds, and water what we want to grow.

No doubt you'd like your child to develop patience, grace, joy, kindness, gentleness. Planting those seeds starts and ends with connection. Connection begins with eye contact. Eye contact says, "Hi. I know you. I like you. I want to know more about you. I am for you. I am with you. No matter what."

Try this experiment today: Walk by your son. Call his name. Look at him with kind eyes and smile. See his entire countenance disarmed, warmed, filled. That is a superpower. Wield it well, my friend.

SEED WISDOM FROM THE OG WISE MAN

> Sow your seed in the morning,
>   and at evening let your hands not be idle,
> for you do not know which will succeed,
>   whether this or that,
>   or whether both will do equally well.
>
> Ecclesiastes 11:6

Have you ever had your best efforts fall flat? In other words, are you a human mother to human children?

Instead of unrealistically expecting perfection, heed these wise words from Solomon, and plant the seeds *all the time*. Look for opportunities to share a sweet moment of eye contact with your boy. If he blows past you and darts toward the puppy, or grumpily demands a snack, take heart! You do not know which seeds are taking root. Plant away.

PRACTICAL AND SIMPLE IDEAS

Create opportunities to gaze into your son's eyes without asking for something. Without "Did you clean your room?" "How much home-work do you have left?" "Go pick up your socks." These are necessary statements for life, of course. But we must also venture beyond the nec-essary, and into the realm of fun and meaningful. Create opportunities for connective (rather than corrective or directive) eye contact. The kind you enjoy with a friend over coffee, or with your spouse on a date.

Here are simple, specific ideas you can use today to increase the amount of eye contact you have with your son.

AGE ZERO TO TWO

1. Peek-a-boo. A classic for good reason. Object permanence is a bizarre concept for little guys. Try this when you're waiting in the drive-thru pharmacy or killing time in the waiting room.

2. Sing a song you love to him. Your littlest dude constantly wants to spend time with mom and to hear from you. He doesn't care how terrible your voice is; he isn't Simon Cowell. Add eye contact and watch him melt.

3. Look into your infant son's eyes while you change him. Tell him about your day, the real meaning of life, the drama with the royals. Ask questions and wait for a coo in reply.

4. Where's the Cheerio? Sitting at a table, put a Cheerio under one of two plastic cups. Lock eyes with your son and move the cups around. Have him guess which cup has the Cheerio. Whenever he guesses correctly, he gets the Cheerio. Be sure to share surprises and reactions with your little one, which is, of course, the best part.

FOR ACTIVE LITTLE PEOPLE

Maybe your toddler is less "precious moments" and more "tiny tyrant." Been there. In that case, you probably spend 70 percent of your time chasing said wild thing. No way he's going to sit while you stare into each other's eyes. Amp up the movement and sensory experiences for this guy and you'll give yourself more opportunities for eye contact.

1. Roaring contest. Take turns roaring at one another. Start with a whisper roar. Alternating turns, get louder and louder. Set the scene here: "Okay, Boris, you and I are lions, and we're trying to scare the other lion away. Let's see if we can keep getting louder and fiercer!"

2. Taste testers. Fill an ice-cube tray or paper plate with various pantry items. One at a time, try a different snack. Ask your child to give a thumbs up or thumbs down after one bite and ten seconds of chewing while looking each other in the eye. You could also leave the question more open if your child is able to verbally express himself. "What do you think of the saltine cracker?" (If self-control is a problem, you could use Easter eggs, or just do one item at a time.) Look at your son while he tastes, listening and ready.

3. Footrace. Stare at each other. When the first person blinks, it's time to race! Keep it close. Exchange reactions with him upon winning and upon losing. Giggles are certain to ensue.

KIDS THREE TO TEN

1. Progressive story. Take turns with each person sharing one to two sentences of a story. Expect lots of nonsense.

2. Charades. Take five minutes before bedtime to act out a word or phrase for your son. Take turns. Use eye contact to show one another you're on the right track, since no words are allowed.

3. Staring contest. You can do this with no blinking or no smiling. Smiling is my favorite. No, I'm not just quoting Buddy the Elf. If you do the kind of staring-into-each-other's-eyes contest where blinking is allowed but not smiling, you will have fun. Alternatively, you could allow blinking and smiling, but no laughing.

Bottom line: Opportunities to increase eye contact with your little guy are *everywhere*. Weave one of these short activities into your day today. You will not regret it.

CONVERSATION

A TOOL TO SERVE HIM FOR LIFE

They are not developing that way of relating where they listen and
learn how to look at each other and hear each other.

—Dean of a New York middle school,
in Sherry Turkle's *Reclaiming Conversation*

It's almost magical how parental conversation appears to influence
the biological growth of the brain.[1]

—John Gabrieli, professor,
MIT's McGovern Institute for Brain Research

Did you know that the biggest indicator of a child's academic success
is the number of words he hears from his primary caregiver between
the ages of zero and three? A landmark study—controlling for income, parental education, and more—showed that the achievement

gap can be attributed to the lack of back-and-forth conversation a child has with his primary caregiver.[2]

This is incredible news for parents, because few to-dos are simpler than talking.

One study showed that month-old infants got excited and sucked more vigorously during nursing when they heard their mother's voice. The same babies did not respond to a stranger's voice.[3]

So talk to your littlest boy as soon as possible. Tell him about your day. Describe what you're doing in the kitchen while he looks on from his baby swing. Verbally respond to his gurgles and coos. This mother-son volley can start from day one and is a critical part of his development. Words are powerful.

"That's great. My child listens to lots of spoken words on TV, YouTube, Netflix. He must be learning a lot!" a mom today might say.

Unfortunately, kids cannot learn functional language from devices. So put down the iPad and pick up your boy. Put him on your lap and open a picture book. This will transform his life over the long term, and the data to support this could not be clearer.

Obviously, if your child is too old to sit on your lap, find a different option. But don't discount reading aloud. I vividly remember my dad reading *The Call of the Wild* aloud to my high school–aged brother. I was legitimately jealous of their bonding time. Choose a book that's *fun*. Talk about the characters, themes, the funny/scary/sad parts.

FORGET EFFICIENCY

With six kids, foster kids, and a broad set of life experiences, we are no strangers to therapy. During one of my first parent-child therapy sessions with a newly placed foster child, I was struck by what I perceived as a lack of efficiency and progress.

"How sweet that we are playing Uno together . . . but maybe we should move on to talk about the feelings, untangle the webs, clear out the hurts and whatnot. Chop-chop." I didn't say this, but I was thinking it.

> The conversations that help our kids sort out their stress, confusion, friendship woes—these opportunities pop up in unexpected and inconvenient places.

So much time was spent building rapport. So much chitchat about nothing. Except that it wasn't about nothing. All of it had a purpose. The games, conversations, back-and-forth turn taking—all of it built trust. It opened the door to talk about the real stuff.

Too often we worship efficiency and progress. In our schedules, in our jobs, and even in our relationships with our kids. When we do, the quiet, seemingly mundane conversational volleys suffer. Then, instead of our kids opening that door to the deeper stuff, they keep it locked. The pearls are inside. But it takes time and conversation to draw them out.

The conversations that help our kids sort out their stress, confusion, friendship woes—these opportunities pop up in unexpected and inconvenient places.

This is the sweet spot where most moms deeply desire to spend time. We want into these heart spaces. But the cost of entrance is time spent in the conversations about nothing and everything. Our trust is earned starting in infancy, and it's woven through the daily, mundane moments.

THE SACRED CONVERSATIONS

"Mom? I feel kind of anxious, and I don't know why," my nine-year-old son said one day while I was folding laundry.

"Hey, thanks for telling me that, bud. It happens to me sometimes too. Let's talk about it. What were you thinking about right before you started feeling this way?"

"Hmm . . . Well, I was thinking about a book report that's due tomorrow. And I have to clean up my room, but I don't want to."

"It makes sense you'd feel stressed out with a lot on your plate. One thing that helps me is to make a plan, and then start on the first thing."

"I think I will do my book report first, then my room," he said.

"Good plan. You got this, buddy. Thanks for talking to me about it."

"Thanks so much, Mom. I feel a lot better."

Obviously, my advice was not rocket science. But there were two major wins I celebrated this day. Number one, that my son had the presence of mind to voice how he was feeling. And number two, that he came to me to talk it through. Whenever this happens, we can celebrate that our kids are trusting us enough to help assess and wrestle through their stresses with them.

And a third win: I stopped what I was doing to give him my full attention.

"The purpose in a man's heart is like deep water, but a man of understanding will draw it out" (Proverbs 20:5 ESV). A mom in pursuit of understanding will draw out the heart of her son.

EVEN THE AWKWARD CONVERSATIONS COUNT!

"I'm cold," our new foster teen said when I suggested a walk. She was only going to be with us for a night or two, and hadn't brought much.

"Do you want to borrow a sweatshirt?" I offered.

"Fine," she said. I handed her a hooded sweatshirt with a Superman logo on it.

"Are you [expletive] serious?"

She was displeased with the sweatshirt, apparently.

"Do you want a different one?"

"I'm going to walk around like, 'Here's this [different expletive].'"

"Well, you won't run into anyone you know. My neighbors have never expressed anything close to those words to me. Plus, we are walking down a country road and you don't know anyone in our city."

"Fine." She rolled her eyes, and we started walking. "So . . . how would you feel if I do some skippity bop while I'm here?"

"What is 'skippity bop'?"

"Drugs."

"I'm gonna go with no on the skippity bop." Full disclosure, I have no recollection of the actual name of the drug. But it was something similarly ridiculous-sounding.

We changed topics, and I asked her about her life. I told her about mine. We ate peanut butter sandwiches, and after a short stay, her social worker picked her up.

That was intense, I thought. *I bet she hated it here. . . . I wish she would've felt more comfortable opening up.*

A few days later, the girl contacted me.

"I really enjoyed staying at your house. Usually I stay in my room on my phone, but I didn't want to stay in my room. I wanted to hang out with you guys. I even surprised myself."

There are three reasons this child didn't stay in her room on her phone, and none of them have to do with incredible parenting skills on my part.

The first is that her phone ran out of battery life, and she didn't have a charger.

The second was peanut butter sandwiches.

The third was adult availability.

Literally any human parent could have provided the sort of atmosphere this child needed. We still keep in touch, talking about life, health, hardship, faith.

THE LITTLE THINGS ARE ACTUALLY THE BIG THINGS

Every time you bear with a Chatty Charlie, genuinely listening and asking follow-up questions—about his very, very long dream about piranhas, his Pokémon card, or his mediocre Lego tower—you are building trust. You're showing him, "I am here. I am your person. I care about what you care about because I love you." Every drawn-out, excruciatingly descriptive story is an opportunity to reinforce your role. Hang in there!

(Also, I'm thinking big picture here. It is totally okay to declare talking breaks. Even the best listeners get fatigued.)

PHONES KILL CONVERSATION

Sherry Turkle has studied technology's impact on society for decades. She shared a concept called the "seven minute rule" in a *New York Times* article. The rule says that a conversation needs seven minutes before it transitions from superficial to deep.[4]

She also says that the presence of a smartphone on a table degrades the quality of conversation. It signals to people, "I'm in this discussion unless my notifications go off," which is a total vibe killer.[5]

While working to create great spaces for conversation with your son, bear this in mind. You don't have to move off the grid forever. But do create intentional spaces for conversation where devices are out of the picture. Car rides, family dinner, even ten minutes after school while enjoying cookies together. Simple, intentional, doable.

IDEAS FOR MORE WORDS AND CONVERSATION STARTERS WITH YOUR KIDS

KIDS ZERO TO THREE

Our tiniest ones have wide ranges of verbal abilities. No matter their ability to respond, the words you speak to them matter!

- Read books.
- Explain where you're driving.
- Use books with objects and words. Point to the objects, say the words, and describe the context for each object.
- Pretend you're in a cooking show and describe your meal prep to the tiny bro in your baby carrier.
- Play this or that. Ask your son which is better, "hamburgers or hot dogs?" "Swimming or biking?" "Chick-fil-A or McDonald's?"

KIDS THREE TO TEN

- Retell stories from when you were a kid. Blow his mind about being older than the internet—if you are. ☺
- Tell him stories about your relatives, where they are from, where they grew up, what they persevered through. (With permission, of course.)
- Tell him about news articles or interesting stories you've read.
- Ask, when did you feel happy today?
- When did you feel sad today?
- What made you laugh today?
- What blew your mind today?
- Did you notice anyone lonely or sad at school today?
- Any dreams last night?
- If you could have any job in the world, what would it be?
- Who is the coolest famous person to you, and why?
- What is your happiest memory?
- What is your hardest memory?
- If a genie could grant you three wishes, what would you pick?
- If you could have any superpower in the world, what would you choose?
- Is there anyone at school you'd like to be closer friends with? Why?
- What qualities do you like to look for in a friend?
- What do you think are your best qualities?
- What is something you want to improve at?
- What is your favorite sport to watch?
- What is your favorite sport to play?
- If you could be transported anywhere, where would you pick?
- What is the most interesting thing you learned today?

- If you could meet any famous person, who would you choose?
- What is the best thing you've ever eaten?
- If you had to choose between invisibility or teleportation, which would you pick?
- What is your dream job? Why?
- Where would you go on vacation if you could choose anywhere?
- What's the last thing that made you laugh really, really hard?
- Name three things you think you're good at.
- Tell me about the best day you've ever had.
- What is the last thing that surprised you?
- What scares you?
- What makes you feel better when you're scared?
- If you couldn't access wi-fi for two weeks, what would you fill your time with?
- What is the coolest animal?
- What do you wish you were an expert in?
- Name someone you know personally whom you have a lot of respect and admiration for.
- What is something you wish your friends knew about you?
- Describe the perfect day.
- What do you think the world will look like in a hundred years?
- Mountains or beach? Why?
- Would you rather fly in a rocket ship or man a submarine?
- If you could instantly have a special talent, what would you choose?
- Dogs or cats?
- Hamsters or lizards?
- Peanut butter or jelly?

- Chocolate desserts or fruity desserts?
- Steak or chicken?
- Apples or oranges?
- Country music or rap?
- Favorite song right now?
- What is a goal you'd like to accomplish in the next year? Five? Ten?
- What is getting in the way of your achieving that goal?
- If we let you have any pet you wanted, what would you choose?
- Tell your son something new you learned.
- Tell him what was hard for you when you were a kid.
- Tell him what you would tell yourself when you were his age.
- Tell him what you admire about him: skills, character, virtues.
- Tell him what your parents were like.
- Tell him the meals you used to eat when you were growing up.
- Tell him how you met his dad.
- Tell him where you've always wanted to travel but have never gone.

So far, we've honed parent-child conversation. This will naturally lay the groundwork to help our kids develop conversation skills with other kids and adults.

But it's also our job to teach our boys how to be great conversationalists with people who don't inherently love twenty-minute stories about their shiny button collections. In addition to giving our kids a leg up in school, work, and their social lives, this can also help them to be less inward focused and love the people around them well.

We've all been stuck in conversations that feel less like an exchange of ideas and more like a monologue from a me-monster. Let's do our kids a favor and show them a better way.

THREE TIPS TO TEACHING YOUR KIDS TO BE GREAT CONVERSATIONALISTS

1. FOCUS ON OTHERS.

Ask questions about the person you're talking with. What are they interested in?

Why? Where do they like to play? What shows do they enjoy?

2. DON'T HOG THE MIC.

Picture a conversation like playing catch. It's cool to hold the mic for a little while, but then you gotta pass it. Nobody likes a ball hog, or a conversation hog.

3. SEEK TO UNDERSTAND.

Use the conversation as an opportunity to learn and understand someone better, not to win an argument.

SKILL-BUILDING SITUATIONS

Instruction is one thing, but giving our boys ample opportunities to practice their skills is another. Ideas for putting our sons in situations to deliberately sharpen these skills:

- Join a club: chess, art, dance, drama.
- Give two siblings a Lego building challenge: "Can you two work together to make a replica of our house?"
- Invite a friend over, and let your kids play and do their thing. For older kids, get smoothie ingredients and baking mixes. Let them make snacks together.

Ask your son whom he enjoys talking with. Does he notice when someone is particularly fun to converse with? What makes them fun?

CONFLICT

AGREEING TO DISAGREE

Men are what their mothers made them.[1]
—Ralph Waldo Emerson,
The Conduct of Life

As iron sharpens iron,
so one person sharpens another.
—Proverbs 27:17

If you've ever found yourself crying into a Starbucks lemon loaf in your minivan at the Target parking lot, welcome to the club.

These episodes happened regularly for me in early motherhood. I'd start my morning brimming with caffeine and optimism. Target run with my toddlers? Yes, please!

Why had I been so hopeful in the first place? Did I have amnesia from last week's trip when a kid puked Skittles in the checkout line? Or the week before, when the boys had a knock-down, drag-out dispute over the piece of lint they found in aisle seven?

Those shopping trips often ended in stress and exhaustion—a result of conflict: Me vs. Child A. Child A vs. Child B. Child B vs. the social standard that pants are required in public. It's one thing to navigate and quell these conflicts at home, but it is quite another to do so in public, when you have the added layer of inner thought: *Is my parenting being judged by the passersby? They don't know he has ADHD/sensory processing issues. They don't know we're weaning from the pacifier.* The perceived need to justify our mothering to any random Judgmental Judy who might be eavesdropping is enough to make your head spin.

Let me encourage you with this: Conflict and our ensuing fear of judgment is an unavoidable part of motherhood for literally everyone. But each instance is an opportunity to teach your sons to navigate this inevitable part of the human experience. It's also an opportunity to turn to the Lord in prayer, with a simple "Help!"

Keep your eye on the ball, and do not care about the haters. Most of the time, haters aren't actually hating. They're often moms who have stood in your shoes and are commiserating through memory. Occasionally you'll meet a real hater. But do you truly value the opinion of someone willing to throw Judge Judy vibes to a mom in the trenches? I do not. If a stranger dishes out judgment pie, do not receive it, my girl. Do not receive it. Just mentally swat it away, and help your boys practice those conflict-navigation skills. Because here is the truth: When your boys encounter conflict, this is not a thwarting of the day's plans; this *is* The Plan. This is what the Lord has prepared for you today. He has prepared this good work for you to walk in. I'm always surprised at the creativity of the chaos He calls me into. But when I do enter in, I take solace in knowing that none of it is out of step with a

> Conflict is noisy, messy, **and** it is an opportunity for mom to roll up her sleeves and give her kids tools to grow in wisdom and maturity.

good, sovereign Father who is sharpening both mother and son through it.

Conflict is noisy, messy, *and* it is an opportunity for mom to roll up her sleeves and give her kids tools to grow in wisdom and maturity. We want to teach our sons that navigating conflict should be genuine, productive, and rooted in love. (This will be a long process.)

THE POWER AND BENEFIT OF CONFLICT

As a recovering passive-aggressivist, my natural bent is to avoid conflict at all costs. A ministry at my church has helped provide words to better understand how we approach conflict. We know Christians are called to be peacemakers. There's the goal. But some of us tend toward peace-faking: "It's fine! No problem here." And others tend toward peace-breaking: "Catch me outside, how 'bout that?" The hope would be that we move closer to our calling of peacemaking, no matter which way our natural inclinations take us. Certainly, there are exceptions, but many moms report that their boys fall into the peace-breaking category more often than the peace-faking.

When I was in college, I remember visiting my boyfriend's fraternity house. We were watching TV in the main living room when two frat brothers began arguing.

"Bro. You still didn't clean up the stain outside our door. That's messed up. Come clean it!"

"Bro. Okay, calm down! Dude," defensive roommate replied.

"I asked you yesterday—that's messed up," broheim said, angrily tossing his roommate a rag.

Roommate scrubbed for several minutes.

"Okay, I did it!" roommate replied, plopping onto the couch.

Thirty seconds passed.

"Bro? Wanna play basketball?" roommate asked without a hint of residual irritation.

"Yeah!" Frat boy jumped up, clearly pumped to shoot hoops
with his buddy.

Within five minutes, these nineteen-year-olds confronted a
wrong, discussed it, resolved it (pun intended), and moved on with
their day. Despite the colorful words I redacted from the exchange,
I was impressed by the young men's directness and willingness to
move on. They were genuine, productive, and rooted in love.

Helping our young boys develop the skills to navigate and grow
from conflict is a massive undertaking. Frankly, most of our work
will not feel productive. But it *is* productive. It is important.

We are working to help our boys use conflict to pursue mutual
understanding. This is hard. Because most of the time when kids
enter conflict, they are not trying to understand, they are trying
to win.

Intentional moms begin when their boys are tiny by teaching
a big-picture biblical worldview. The tools I'm about to share are
simpler to understand in that framework. But even if these ideas
don't land initially, be encouraged that you're planting seeds and
watering. Fruit is on the horizon!

Here are a few Bible verses and stories you can share to teach
your young boys practically about navigating conflict productively,
and biblically.

Biblical example: "As iron sharpens iron, so one person sharpens another"
(Proverbs 27:17).

Demonstrate: If you have a knife sharpener, show your son how it works. Explain
that both blades are sharp. Show him how it makes unpleasant noise sometimes
while sharpening. (Kind of like how he and his brother sound when they argue.)
But if it's done well, even if it's noisy, it can produce something very good, making
the knife more effective than it was before the sharpening.

Takeaway: When we conflict with siblings or friends, it can make us better! Like
knives. But we need to work to conflict productively, and not destructively. Two
sharp objects could easily break one another if they aren't thoughtfully and care-
fully interacting. The same is true for us with our words and actions.

Biblical example: Joseph was a little extra, bragging to his brothers about a dream in which he was the boss of everybody. Joseph's brothers could have chosen to have a conversation about their irritation with Joseph. Instead, those ruthless bullies sold him into slavery! Then they lied to their dad that he'd been killed. Yikes. Probably a result of years of built-up anger, and not working through conflict productively.

Demonstrate: Ask, "Have you ever been so mad about a bunch of little things that you finally exploded and did something bad like yell or scream or hit?" If you're willing, share about a time you blew up after pent-up frustration. Share how things might have gone better if you had addressed each frustration at the time it arose.

Takeaway: When we avoid conflict with our siblings and friends, stress and anger can build up. Sometimes sin overflows and creates a situation that's much worse than if we'd been willing to face the conflict the first time around.

Biblical example: "How can you say to your brother, 'Brother, let me take out the speck that is in your eye,' when you yourself do not see the log that is in your own eye? You hypocrite, first take the log out of your own eye, and then you will see clearly to take out the speck that is in your brother's eye" (Luke 6:42 NASB).

Demonstrate: With your back facing your son, hold a big log or a giant object like it's coming out of your eye. Turn to him and pretend not to notice your own giant obstruction, telling him, "Wow, you have a tiny little thing in your eye. You really need to get that taken care of." Adopt a judgmental tone. If you don't have a log lying around, try putting a big piece of chocolate over your front tooth. Turn to your son, smile big, and tell him, "Wow, you have a little dot of black pepper in your tooth. That's embarrassing for you." He will probably be pretty quick to see that the joke is on you. Giggle together about how silly you are. Then tell him you actually got this idea from Jesus, who made this joke to His followers. Share the verse with him and remind him that we're better together.

Takeaway: Don't be a speck hunter if you've got a giant plank blocking your view. We are called to gently tell each other when we have junk to deal with that we can't see ourselves. But we are wise to take care of our own junk before helping someone with theirs.

Biblical example: "The heart is more deceitful than all else and is desperately sick; who can understand it?" (Jeremiah 17:9 NASB).

Demonstrate: Share about a time when you really thought you were right about a fact or argument but found out later that you were wrong. Or tell your son about how Judas walked around with Jesus for years, following Him and learning from Him. Then he betrayed Jesus, turning Him in to the people who hated Him, just for a sack of money. After he realized how bad a choice that was, he tried to give the money back. But it was too late.

Takeaway: Because sin is in our hearts, we all are capable of being wrong, selfish, or mean. That's why we need God's Word, to show us when we are wrong. God also uses His people sometimes to show us when we are wrong. Are you listening with a soft heart in case God is trying to tell you that your heart is being led by sin instead of by God?

TOOLS TO NAVIGATE CONFLICT

1. Conflict is like when you're going on a bear hunt and you come up to a lake. You can't go under it. You can't go around it. You gotta go through it. Pack your backpack with the tools you need to go through it!
2. Don't talk until the other person is finished. Take turns.
3. Listen to understand the other person.
4. Own your part of the dispute. Even if you are responsible for only 10 percent of the conflict, own that 10 percent completely.[2]
5. Specifically apologize for the part you are able to apologize for.
6. If appropriate, hug it out.

Some kids will be receptive to these tools and verses from the get-go. Others will make you feel like you are banging your head against a wall every time you try to explain how to navigate conflict *again*. Remember: God has called you to mother this exact boy, at this exact time. He knows your heart, and He knows your son's heart. He calls you to be faithful to your job as mother, not to guarantee that all your teaching sticks in his heart and mind. That part is above your pay grade. If firstborn Billy made flower crowns for his teachers at recess but second-born Rupert is starting mini Fight Club at recess, stress not. Children are wired differently; you're not a failure. But you *are* called to tune in and lovingly correct, redirect, and teach your child how to use conflict for good. Done well, your boys' conflicts can help slough off the junky aspects of their personalities.

YOUR EFFORTS ARE NEVER IN VAIN

"Mine!" my four-year-old daughter yelled at my three-year-old son.

"No, mine!" my son yelled back.

I was no stranger to sibling squabbles. I was also constantly trying to encourage these growing kids to work out their own disagreements. *This is a perfect opportunity*, I thought. So I rolled up my sleeves and stood alongside my dueling preschoolers. *I'm not going to take the toy this time. I'm going to help them find common ground.*

"Okay, Jack. What if you tell your sister, 'Let's take turns,'" I suggested.

"MINE!" Pint-sized Jack bowed up and doubled down.

Not receptive to my suggestion. Time to appeal to the older and wiser sister.

"Selah," I tried, full of optimism and hope. "What if you said, 'You have five minutes, I have five minutes'?" I may as well have been talking to a wall.

"JACKY!!! NOOOO!" Selah screamed.

I continued my futile attempts to help them establish common ground. Unity. Love.

"You poopoo!" Jack busted out the harshest burn in his toolbox.

Welp, this is not going the way I hoped, I thought. My efforts looked to be very much in vain, culminating with big sister clocking little brother upside his head.

"Aw, so close," I lied, removing the toy and scooping big sister into timeout.

I relayed the story to David when he came home from work. We laughed at my failed attempts to teach conflict-resolution skills to tiny angry people.

Maybe my plan was too lofty for the kids to grasp at their ages. Maybe you're similarly wondering if your lessons are going way over your kids' heads. But I do not regret my attempts to impart reasonableness to dysregulated mini humans. Because that's exactly what they needed. Their conflict was genuine. It might not have looked productive at the time, but when you view it as one of five thousand examples of how *not* to conflict, you realize that it was indeed a productive experience, despite what your eyes are telling you. A mom who remains regulated and calm demonstrates love, even in the midst of chaos.

We have no way to know if the teaching and training will finally sink in on repetition number five, or number five thousand. So we continue onward, trusting that God works all things out for our good and His glory.

SELF-FORGETFULNESS

HIGHLIGHT SIBLING ACCOMPLISHMENT (SIDE-EYEING YOU, CAIN . . .)

Humility is the most difficult of all virtues to achieve; nothing dies harder than the desire to think well of oneself.

—T. S. Elliot, "Shakespeare and the Stoicism of Seneca"[1]

"Listen, dummy, the Cheetos are mine! And stop looking at me!"

"You stop looking at ME!" little brother snipped, lunging at the bag of Cheetos in his brother's hand. According to the rules of car-pool sibling conflict, Cheeto thievery was an act of war. Two more siblings joined in the conflict.

"NO! You're so stupid!" Elbows flew. Verbal shots were fired.

Rage oozed from the passenger seats of my parked car. These kids were hungry, grumpy, and starting to remind me of squabbling knuckleheads Harry and Lloyd from *Dumb and Dumber*. I blinked long and hard, desperately wishing my oldest child's practice would finish so that we could drive home and give these brawling bros some space. If my minivan had an ejection seat that could launch me out of my sunroof and into a hammock with a nice little umbrella drink, I'd have pushed the button.

It had been a long afternoon. We still had five more minutes before practice ended and my ejection seat hadn't been invented yet, so I was forced to choose a different solution.

"Okay, listen up." I had an idea. "You're going to say your favorite thing about the person next to you. Who's going first?"

Silence.

"Okay, Jack. You're going first. Tell us your favorite thing about Mason."

"Mason's hair is crazy today," said Jack, trying to pull a switcheroo. I ignored him.

"Mason, what's your favorite thing about Jack?"

Mason thought for a moment. "Jack is really good at sports . . . and he is good at making food." Mason was right. Those are two of Jack's strengths. And his genuine reply silenced the car. Ten seconds later, Jack spoke up.

"Can I get a redo?" Jack asked sheepishly.

"Sure," I said.

"I really like that Mason tries new things. He invents cool machines that he'll build with random supplies from the backyard. He's creative," his voice softened.

I glanced in the rearview mirror. Mason was beaming, obviously touched by words of affirmation from big brother.

"I agree, Jack. That's a great quality. Your turn, Carter. Favorite thing about Elaina?"

Carter paused. Complimenting the person he had just argued with? That can feel like death. (Because it is! Death to self.)

A series of non-responses popped up, which I ignored, skipping to the next person each time. When the smug answers fell flat, the kids stopped offering them. Instead, they used their next opportunity to say something genuine. They felt the climate of the car change simply by adjusting their postures and words—from cutting down to building up.

I bit my tongue on the drive home, sparing the kids the lecture I desperately wanted to give them. I showed instead of told. They sat in silence. I knew they were thinking about the last ten minutes. Mission accomplished.

That afternoon in the school parking lot, we broke the Harry and Lloyd cycle. And it started with a nudge and a prompt from mom. These boys moved from self-focused to others-focused, and that shift quelled the fighting and made everyone happier. But they wouldn't have gotten there on their own. They needed mama to lead them. Often we find ourselves surrounded by the stress and chaos of our boys acting contrary to the ways we teach. Maybe you're like me and wish for an ejection seat, or sneak off to hide in the pantry with a Snickers bar. Maybe you yell, discipline without training, or check out entirely. But the golden opportunities to help lead your boys onto a better path are there waiting for you. It'd be easier to see it if the path wasn't covered in off-putting behavior. This is why many parents check out at the ripest moment. Rolling up your sleeves to invest here is really, really hard. Do it anyway. Intercept your kids at their worst. When you do, you're helping them to create new neural pathways in the places that matter most.

Can I encourage you with a little dose of reality? I attempt solutions like this all the time. They're not all successful. Some days I'm working with a 90 percent failure rate. But if you're attempting to move your boy into a mindset where he isn't putting himself first, you're going to hit failure walls. On this day, I tossed some wet spaghetti at the wall, and a few strands stuck. Success!

Here's the secret: No one has perfect kids. We know this, because all of them are human beings with various types of sin proclivities. And so are we. If anyone is fronting like they're not in that boat, well, I'm not super interested in their advice. I'm interested in how flawed moms take flawed kids and humbly pursue God with the freedom purchased for us via the gospel. Failure is part of the journey. So if you try this with your boys and it falls flat—great job! You're on the journey. You'll have zillions of opportunities to try again.

LEAD YOUR LITTLE LAMB, MARY

Have you ever watched young kids show sheep at the county fair? I didn't grow up in 4-H, so a recent experience at the fair was new to me. I watched a dozen three- to eight-year-old kids enter the ring, each leading a sheep by a short leash. Their job was to direct their sheep around the pen. Stand when it was time to stand, walk when it was time to walk. Most of the kids led their sheep by a short rope. But two older boys in the competition didn't use a leash at all. Instead, these boys stood alongside their sheep, holding out their hand. The sheep nestled its chin into their boy's hand. The boy led his sheep around the pen like this. When the boy walked, the sheep walked. When the boy stopped, his sheep stopped. Those boys kept their eyes on the judge, awaiting instruction. They'd clearly spent time building rapport and bonding with their sheep. These sheep trusted their boys. They wanted to follow.

The more time and effort you spend building your relationships with your boys, the more they will follow you. When you lead selflessly, they will want to emulate that. For now, with our young boys, we still use the lead, prompting them to come back to the right way. But over time, as you patiently, repeatedly prompt them back to the right path, you are creating and growing those habits.

> The more time and effort you spend building your relationships with your boys, the more they will follow you. When you lead selflessly, they will want to emulate that.

YOU'RE THE BEST PERSON TO TEACH SELFLESSNESS TO YOUR SON

It just so happens that your son's mom is the perfect person for this job. You are the most important woman in his life (for now), and your job is to expand his capacity for high-quality relationships. His ability to make and sustain relationships depends on his posture toward the people around him. Is he able to consider the needs of others? Celebrate them? Honor them? Can self-forgetfulness and true humility be taught? Absolutely.

I'm not talking about self-loathing, that sackcloth-and-ashes thing. I'm talking about the true version of humility—thinking of yourself less, rather than thinking less of yourself. The kind of humility that gushes out of a person who knows he is valued, loved, treasured. (Ahem, first few chapters.) He's not wondering if he is awesome; he knows it because you're a mom who makes sure that he does. That person is secure in his belonging. So secure that he wants to go out and lift up the people around him. Look, I know this sounds impossible for tiny me-monsters. But that's what makes your daily, hourly commitment to him even more beautiful.

On the bedrock of our first few chapters, we are calling our boys to level up. If we want to raise boys who love their neighbors as themselves, let's equip them to do it!

RESEARCH SUPPORTS YOUR EFFORTS

Whatever you practice, you become good at.

An entire generation of boys are markedly less motivated, less interested in relationships, less likely to marry and have kids. But because they're playing video games forty-plus hours per week, they're really good at that. They're not practicing real skills they'll need in the real world. They're turning inward, disregarding the people around them.

The failure-to-launch epidemic is real for young men. Fifty-eight percent of men ages eighteen to twenty-four live at home with their parents.[2] These are men who have potential, but it's wasting away as they game alone in their parents' basements, squandering their God-given gifts.

Did you know that the evidence linking video games to antisocial behaviors is about as strong as evidence linking secondhand smoke to the risk of lung cancer?[3]

The prevention of this disease is more fundamental than limiting screen time, although that is a massive aspect of it. Our sons need to see the world outside of themselves. If your son thinks that the point of life is his own comfort and entertainment, he is on the same path as the young men who are squandering their potential on entertainment. They are living under the false idea that the hero in their story is themselves. They are missing the real life and relationships God has in store for them.

WHAT ABOUT HIS SELF-ESTEEM?

The correlation between a boy's self-esteem related to a subject and his performance in that subject is zero.

What?

I know. This blew my mind. I *know* I perform better at a subject when I'm more confident in that subject. I've also seen this proven in my daughters. And research supports that—for females. But for males, that's not the case. Dr. Leonard Sax, author of *Boys Adrift* and practicing physician, says that self-esteem has value for girls that it does not have for boys.[4] Instead, he says, competition is a better motivator for boys to perform well. A coach who has worked with both male and female athletes for years told Dr. Sax that girls must be encouraged, or else they'll give up. This is not the case for boys. She says that athletically talented boys tend to overestimate their abilities. "You have to tell that hotshot that he may have some talent, but he's not nearly as good as he thinks he is. He still has a lot to learn. He's going to need to put in a lot of work if he wants to make it to the next level."[5]

Build up your son's identity as a child of God, and help him see that his unique gifts are to be used to benefit the people around him. Self-esteem will take care of itself.

PRACTICAL IDEAS FOR TEACHING SELFLESSNESS TO TINY TYRANTS

Let's get practical. Here are five simple ideas for helping your little man to see outside himself, and to forge some neural pathways contrary to the idea that the world revolves around him.

"You Are Special" plate. Have you seen this red plate? It's ceramic and has beautiful white lettering that says, "You Are Special Today." On birthdays we bring it out for the birthday child. Everyone else uses a normal plate that night. Except the birthday kid. You'd be surprised by how much excitement a dinner plate can elicit.

Use this plate to invite your son into being others-focused. Ask him to be the Plate Opportunity Spotter for siblings. "Can you help me? I want to remember to honor our family members when they do something special. If you notice that one of your siblings scores a goal, or earns an academic award, or goes above and beyond to help the people around them, can you let me know? We can surprise them with the special plate that night at dinner."

Dinnertime encouragement. Quell the elbow-nudging by announcing that the family is going to celebrate something specific about the person to their right. Mom or dad can start this one, then go around the table.

Share short biographical accounts of selfless people. When your kids want to watch a show during the weekdays and you don't typically allow it, make one exception: Torchlighters. You can find these videos online to stream, or as DVDs at your local library. Each animated episode highlights a hero of the Christian faith: John Wesley, Corrie ten Boom, Jim Elliot, and many more.

Counterexamples. Sometimes it's easier for our boys to spot examples of failure. Share a few familiar biblical examples of men who blew it because they were selfishly concerned with their own interests. (Abraham pimping out his wife to save his own skin. Judas selling out Jesus for a few bucks.)

Serve with your kids. Ask your local church if they need any help that would be feasible to include your son in. Our city has a mission where families without stable housing can come and stay for a little while, until they are on their feet. We volunteer with our kids during their church service. My son and I serve in the nursery. It doesn't get much simpler than holding babies. Show your boys that service is an important rhythm of your life, and makes an eternal impact. You could also do a simple neighborhood trash pickup or ask your local pregnancy resource center if they need volunteers with sorting, organizing, or miscellaneous family friendly projects.

#3 AUTHORITY

The world: "My three-year-old and I share authority. *My* truth might say that bedtime is 8 p.m., but *his* truth says bedtime is whenever the sugar crash hits. I always count to three waiting for him to do what I ask, but never enforce a consequence when he doesn't. Yes, we are both exhausted all day, and his personality is insufferable, but I want to raise a son who can assert himself."

Mission-minded boy mom: "My son must respect me as his authority, even when I'm tired. Through my authority, he is learning to respect future teachers, bosses, and women in general. There will be plenty of time when he is grown for us to have a relationship that looks more like a friendship."

Your son needs his mama to exercise the authority God has given her. How you interact with him as teacher, coach, leader—this is the foundation for how he will relate to all authority in his life. What makes it trickier: The natural bent of our boys is to defy that authority. We are in this thing for the long haul, and we will not relinquish our duty in the face of difficulty. As your son grows into his teen and tween years, your authority will begin to diminish, from commander to coach, and eventually to mentor as he spreads those wings and flies the nest one day. But when your boy is small, you must teach him a foundational understanding for authority. The next three chapters, "Respecting Authority," "Natural Consequences," and "Waiting," will provide tools for helping you to instill a respect for authority in the heart of your son.

RESPECTING AUTHORITY

BEYOND "BECAUSE I SAID SO"

It's respect for your parents that is the basis for every other kind of respect and every other kind of authority.

—Tim Keller in Bret Eckleberry's "Honor Your Father and Mother," *Focus on the Family*[1]

He is on the path of life who heeds instruction,
But he who ignores reproof goes astray.

—Proverbs 10:17 NASB

"Mom! Zack's friend just tried to light our tablecloth on fire!"

"What?! Where are Zack and his friend now?" Emily didn't want to host this playdate in the first place. But now she was regretting it more than that time she got bangs in the ninth grade.

"Now?" Emily's daughter looked around. "Oh, there they are. Zack's friend caught a lizard and he's . . . trying to put him in our freezer? Ew!" Emily's twelve-year-old daughter stared at her mom, wide-eyed.

Emily couldn't believe how difficult her son's friend was. They were thirty minutes into a three-hour playdate. He couldn't have been allowed to do these things at his own house, right? Certainly she wasn't crazy in expecting a third-grader to function without helicopter supervision at someone else's house? Playdates typically meant *less* parenting required of her. The kids kept out of trouble, building Lego, playing a board game, refraining from pyrotechnics.

"Hey, guys." Emily had abandoned her laundry pile and returned to the kitchen. "No reptiles in the freezer, and no playing with fire, okay?" *Like, duh.*

The friend closed the freezer without making eye contact with Emily. "We're bored," he said.

Boring is as boring does, is what Emily would have responded to her own child, summoning her best Forrest Gump voice. Alas, these silly replies were off the table for friends, no matter how obnoxious they were acting. Emily was beginning to wish Zack had invited a different friend over.

"Well, it's a beautiful day out. You could play basketball, take a walk, ride bikes?" Emily tried.

"Nah," the boy walked out of the room, grabbing a cookie on his way out the door. Without asking. *With lizard-germ hands.* Emily's blood began to boil.

Zack turned to his mom, face red, and eyes that said, "Sorry, Mom. This is awkward."

Two hours later (our fire extinguisher on standby but out of sight), the friend's mom finally drove up.

"Son, we need to go," she said sweetly, looking at her watch.

"No, I'm still playing," he said, running to the trampoline with Zack and his sister.

"Okay. Ten jumps, then let's go," she said. But the boy was long gone. His mom watched him jump for nearly ten minutes, intermittently requesting that he get off the trampoline. The boy ignored his mom every time. Emily watered her garden nearby, making small talk with the other mom while feeling embarrassed on her behalf.

As the minutes passed, this mom looked visibly stressed out and defeated. "Are you okay?" Emily asked.

"Yeah, it's just that we have my niece's rehearsal dinner tonight. We're supposed to be there in an hour. We still need to go home and get dressed," she said as she looked at her watch.

"Oh, yeah, you really need to go!" Emily realized that this mom had lost all control of the situation and genuinely didn't know how to get her child to leave. She stepped in to help. "Hey, Zack, come on over here; your friend has to leave."

Zack and his sister hopped off the trampoline, jogging toward the moms.

"I'll race you guys there!" Emily's daughter said, trying to help.

"Yeah, right. I'll lose to a girl!" the friend said, shoving her.

"Ow!" She tripped and fell to the ground. Zack stopped running to help his sister up.

"Dude! What was that?" Zack asked. The friend ignored him.

Emily turned to the boy's mom, waiting for her to enforce some kind of correction, or at least signal embarrassment.

"Oh, jeez," the mom said under her breath. "Boys, right?"

WHY ARE BOYS ACTING LIKE THIS?

Unfortunately, this experience has become too common. Maybe you've been in Emily's shoes before. You've volunteered in the classroom, hosted the playdate, watched the soccer games, and you've seen it—boys ignoring the teacher, mom, coach. Why? *Because if we don't require our sons to respect authority, they will not do it.*

When moms don't enforce this basic requirement, we undermine our ability to parent, protect, and teach. Fast-forward a few years, and you'll find a generation of boys who can't complete schoolwork, hold down a job, or lead a family.

Teaching them to respect authority is the most fundamental building block of raising boys who love and obey God. They're only under our authority for eighteen years—if that. And various seasons will have them under the authority of coaches, teachers, and bosses. But they're under God's authority for their entire lives. Helping our boys to love God and their neighbors starts with the fundamental concept that they answer to someone above them.

THE POWER OF A PARENT WHO MODELS OBEDIENCE TO GOD

The real issue in the garden of Eden was that Eve wanted independence from God's authority. She wanted to make the rules. She listened to the enemy's lie that God was holding out on her. She looked at the fruit God told her not to eat. She saw that it looked good in *her* eyes. She valued her own assessment over God's authority. So she sought autonomy from God.

All human sin stems from our desire for autonomy from God's authority. "I don't want to do what God says. I want to do it my way."

This isn't unique to our boys. We suffer from the same sin disease they do; we're just better at hiding it.

The most powerful way to help our kids understand God as our authority is to live out obedience ourselves. What do we do when our preferences collide with God's instruction? Talk about this with your kids. Share about times when you chose to obey God's authority, or a time when you didn't.

Mom and Dad attend church on Sundays because God's Word tells us not to forsake the gathering.[2] Maybe some mornings you'd rather sleep in, but you get up and go anyway. Share that wrestle. "I love God, and I love worshiping Him. This morning, though, I just didn't feel like getting up. But I'm so glad I obeyed Him anyway. I'm always glad when I choose His way instead of mine."

Or maybe your example is a little grittier.

"A driver cut me off today. It took all of my self-control not to give him a piece of my mind at the stoplight. I know God doesn't

> Don't underestimate the power of wrestling against your flesh in front of your kids. We serve an efficient God. He doesn't waste any of our struggles.

want His people screaming at other drivers, even when they're bad drivers. So guess what? I smiled and gave the guy a thumbs-up instead. *Then,* I realized he looked familiar. It was my boss's husband! Good thing I didn't do it my way, huh? God's way is always better."

This is the fun part, because we get to live out the Christian life for our kids to see. Don't underestimate the power of wrestling against your flesh in front of your kids. We serve an efficient God. He doesn't waste any of our struggles. He sometimes even uses them to show our kids what a life of obedience, grace, and repentance looks like.

BE DISCERNING WHEN YOU TAKE ADVICE; CONFIDENTLY REJECT UNWISE COUNSEL

One last note about mothering in the world of social media. We've never had access to so many varying opinions about the "right way" to parent our kids. I've seen so many online accounts share videos that say things like "Instead of telling your kids, 'Don't do that,' or 'No, you can't . . .' tell your kids, 'After this, then you can do that.' This way you can avoid negative or prohibitive words."

Um. What?

"Jeroboam, after you can manifest yourself into a car and run 65 miles per hour, then you can dart into the street, okay?"

"Hey, little Boaz, after you punch your brother in his stomach, then you can sit in the namaste chair to think about how those vibrations felt in your chakras, okay?"

I'll pass on that style of parenting.

For the Christian mom, the Bible is our authority in everything, especially parenting. Every Bible translation includes clear commands, full of "Do this, don't do that" instructions. How is it helpful to our kids to not convey those? It isn't. It sounds more like a strategy to avoid telling your child something they don't want to hear, much to their disservice.

"Jeroboam, you may NOT run into the street. If you do, you could get hit by a car and die. If you disobey me when I tell you not to do that, you will get a consequence you do not like. I love you too much to allow you to disobey this rule without correcting you." (Then you sure as heck better follow through on that.)

"Boaz, it is not okay to punch, hit, or hurt anybody. God says to love your neighbor. Hitting is not loving. You will face a consequence when you disobey Mom's rule and God's command. I love you too much to allow you to do this."

Correction is a great way of connecting all the dots you've been plotting for your son about the truth of who God is, and why we need Jesus. I've explained to my young kids many times through the course of correction and discipline that I discipline them because God tells me to. God is my authority. God tells moms that they must teach, train, and discipline their kids. If I allowed my kids to keep doing things that God calls sin, I would be disobeying God. The most important thing I do in my life is obey God. And the deepest desire of my heart is for my kids to love and obey God. Check out this passage from Hebrews 12:5–11 (NIrV). Share it with your son through the course of discipline.

> "My son, think of the Lord's training as important.
> Do not lose hope when he corrects you.
> The Lord trains the one he loves.
> He corrects everyone he accepts as his son."

Put up with hard times. God uses them to train you. He is treating you as his children. What children are not trained by their parents? God trains all his children. But what if he doesn't train you? Then you are not really his children. You are not God's true sons and daughters at all. Besides, we have all had human fathers who trained us. We respected them for it. How much more should we be trained by the Father of spirits and live! Our parents trained us for a little while. They did what they thought was best. But God trains us for our good. He does this so we may share in his holiness. No training seems pleasant at the time. In fact, it seems painful. But later on it produces a harvest of godliness and peace. It does this for those who have been trained by it.

Thankfully, the Bible allows *a lot* of latitude in parenting style. (Homeschool? Organic produce? Bedtimes? You do you!) But where the instruction is clear and universal, we must adhere to it. So when Deuteronomy 6 tells us to teach His commands to our children diligently, then we will do it.

BIBLE VERSES ABOUT GOD'S AUTHORITY TO MEMORIZE WITH OUR SONS

What pleases the LORD more?
Burnt offerings and sacrifices, or obeying the LORD?
It is better to obey than to offer a sacrifice.
It is better to do what he says than to offer the fat of rams.

1 Samuel 15:22 NIrV

Have respect for God and obey his commandments.
This is what he expects of all human beings.
God will judge everything people do.
That includes everything they try to hide.
He'll judge everything, whether it's good or evil.

Ecclesiastes 12:13–14 NIrV

How terrible it will be for anyone who argues with their
Maker!
They are like a broken piece of pottery lying on the
ground.
Does clay say to a potter,
"What are you making?"
Does a pot say,
"The potter doesn't have any skill"?

Isaiah 45:9 NIrV

Children, obey your parents as believers in the Lord. Obey them because it's the right thing to do. Scripture says, "Honor your father and mother." That is the first commandment that has a promise. "Then things will go well with you. You will live a long time on the earth."

Ephesians 6:1–3 NIrV

Children, obey your parents in everything. That pleases the Lord.

Colossians 3:20 NIrV

> My son, do not hate the LORD's training.
>   Do not object when he corrects you.
> The LORD trains those he loves.
>   He is like a father who trains the son he is pleased with.

Proverbs 3:11–12 NIrV

TEACHING OBEDIENCE

We get to teach our son:

- That he is required to obey God, Mom, Dad, teachers, coaches, authority generally.
- Why his heart wants to disobey. We all have sin in our hearts that wants us to make decisions without God.
- That there is forgiveness for his disobedience. (Thank You, Jesus!)
- That he can't use forgiveness as an excuse to keep disobeying.

The hardest part is that we must teach this constantly, and we won't always be able to see growth. But we will continue to plant seeds, trusting that God is doing the heart work. The stuff way above our pay grade. We teach our boys diligently, knowing that we'll be held to account for how we steward our time and influence with our boys.

SIMPLE AND PRACTICAL

Don't make a joke out of disobedience. If you call your toddler to the dinner table, and he runs away laughing, don't turn it into a game. Respond with, "This is not a game. Right now you need to obey Mommy. Come sit down." If he continues to reject your authority, he needs a consequence.

Enforce consequences. Losing a treat, going to bed early, missing out on a movie, losing a playdate—whatever makes sense for your family—our boys need consequences for disobedience. When they are small, the consequences are relatively small. Our hope is that they figure out obedience when the stakes are low, and not down the road when juvie is on the horizon. This is why the most loving thing you can do for your small boys is require them to obey your God-given authority.

Don't sweat the tantrums. Tantrums are inevitable if your child hears "no." If you're at the grocery store, and you decline your child's request for a treat or toy, and he proceeds to tantrum? Do not give in. Do not. Show him you will leave that store, and in fact, he will not get his after-dinner treat now. You do not negotiate with terrorists. Stand your ground, mama. And know there's a high chance that more than half the customers in that store have walked in your shoes. They understand. And the rest of them are probably grateful that you're not raising an entitled child. (I always told my kids, "The second you throw a tantrum you've turned my answer to a definite no. A tantrum is the quickest way to never get what you want.")

Back up the teachers. When your son is under the care of a babysitter or later a teacher, make sure he knows that he is expected to obey their authority. I've lost track of how many conversations I've had with teachers who've told me, "It's hard to manage the classroom because we don't have parental support like we used to. Kids goof off, and the parents defend it. What recourse do I have?" If a teacher reports disrespect or disobedience, back them up. For their sake, and also for your son's. (You don't even have to agree with everything a teacher does in order to support them as your son's authority! Obviously, if there are glaring problems, you should respectfully have that conversation with them. But even that situation would be an opportunity to live out respect and honor toward people in authority.) Every authority in his life presents an opportunity to honor God.

Talk to your kids. Give your boys context for why they're required to obey you, and God. Here are a few conversation starters so they can think through the whys of obeying authority.

- "Our authorities have drawn lane lines on the freeway. . . . What do you think would happen if we erased all of the lines, and people could drive wherever they wanted?"
- "Look at those posted speed limits. What do you think would happen if they took that away and everyone could drive the speed that felt right in their own heart?"
- "What would happen if you went into the classroom and the teacher's direction to the class was, 'Everyone may do whatever he wants today! Follow your heart.' Do you think the class would learn anything? Do you think that would be good for the students?"

DOCILE DONNIE AND RUDE RUDY

Here is the reality: Some boys take to obeying authority more easily than others.

With a large sample size of children who have come in and out of our home through foster care and my womb, I promise you no two have been the same. Some take very easily to my instruction, while others tend more toward the "Shut up, lady" personality type. (Kids say the darndest things.)

If you're anything like me, the most crippling and frustrating part of parenting a Rude Rudy is when you're working your leggings off, diligently training that child up, requiring his obedience at every turn. You're like, lighting candles and requesting masses for the kid, and you're not even Catholic. But little Rudy has the thickest skull and hardest heart you've ever seen.

Meanwhile, that mom, Self-Righteous Sally over there, happened to pop out a Docile Donnie. If little Donnie isn't on stage singing in the church choir, he's bringing his teacher cookies that he woke up early to bake after treating his mom to breakfast in bed. Even worse, whenever you compliment Sally about Donnie, she's always like, "We just work hard to teach him right and wrong," condescension oozing from her smile. That is so great for you and Donnie, Sally. But what Sally doesn't know is that not all boys are Donnies. There is no universe in which, if you repeated the instructions one more time, Rudy would also bring you breakfast in bed. (Well, maybe if you weren't such a bad mom, according to Sally's way of thinking.)

My friend. All children have a different posture and proclivity to sin, and specifically in submitting to authority. You're working with the lump of clay you got. God gave you the kid He gave you to sharpen you *and* him. Okay? I say this confidently because if the good Lord only gave me one child, and it was one of my docile ones, I'd probably (wrongly) judge the moms of Rude Rudys. But in His infinite wisdom, God gave me a generous mix of both. Blood, sweat, and tears have shaved off the parts of my boys prone to defiance. And guess what? In my house, we have a kid who continues to struggle with those proclivities. So we return to this battlefield daily. And while we are on that field, the Lord reminds me that I have my own issues, too, not wanting to trust His authority in allowing Rudy to continue to act turd-like. God is so efficient that He parents us *while* we parent them. He roots out our fear of man in the process. (And why are we so concerned that Sally may not understand that we're not slacking—we just have a hard kid? Why is her opinion so weighty when the God of the universe knows our heart and our workload?)

We are in this motherhood thing for the long haul. And we're each working with different dough. So let faithfulness—not results—be your metric here.

Do not be discouraged if your kid's got a heart that bucks authority. Just take note. This is the boy God has specifically chosen for you to love, teach, and discipline. Look at that—He has called *you* up for this massive task! He ain't calling Sally over there. Not for this wild heart. But He has called YOU. You're willing, and He wants to do a great work in and through you as you submit to His authority, by requiring your son to submit to yours.

The road will be messy.

The vice principal might call.

YOU WILL FAIL IN EMBARRASSING WAYS.

But this is not the end of your mothering story. This is just the beginning. And taking up the fight for the heart of your boy is the mark of a faithful mom in pursuit of God. A faithful mom teaches her son to obey her, and she does it every day. You are planting critically important seeds in the heart of your son. Do it often. Watch for glimpses of Rudy submitting to your authority, the coach's, the teacher's, God's. Call it out when you see it. "Rudy, I noticed when you really didn't want to run a lap at soccer. But the coach told you to do it, so you did it. That was hard. I was so proud of you, son. Did you know that when you obey authority, it glorifies God? Even when it's something seemingly small like that. Well done, Rudy. . . . Rudy! Rudy! Rudy!"

NATURAL CONSEQUENCES

LET HIM REAP WHAT HE SOWS

The worst thing you can do for those you love is the things they could and should do themselves.

—Attributed to Abraham Lincoln[1]

Once upon a time, there was a four-year-old boy who fingerpainted the bathroom walls. I know, some mom's blood pressure is already rising. But wait, it gets worse. The boy wasn't painting with paint. He was painting with, well, something one might find (and leave) in the bathroom. Something that should never be used as paint.

After several incidents of this, mom decided she'd had enough. "Son," she said, "this is disgusting. I've told you time and again that this is not okay. Now you need to deal with the consequences of your bad choices." Mom handed several wet, soapy paper towels to the boy. "Your turn," she said.

After every previous "painting," the boy would say he was sorry, but never showed true remorse. Then mom would clean the mess because she wanted it done right.

This time was different. The small boy looked at the brown wall, then at the wet towels, then at his mom. He was horrified at the task before him. "But . . ." he said, "this is gross! It is so yucky . . . I wish I never did this!"

"Exactly," mom replied.

Thirty minutes of elbow grease later, this boy decided that would be the last time he fingerpainted the bathroom walls.

THE BEST WAY TO HELP HIM: DON'T RESCUE HIM

Natural consequences are mom's most powerful tools for teaching her son how the world works, and that he has the power to set himself up for success—or failure. Allowing consequences to play out reinforces the reality that the world does not revolve around our kids. It helps them understand through experience that a larger force has set up a natural order, whether we like it or not.

This concept is becoming increasingly foreign in our culture, where personal preference trumps God's design. Moms today need to work harder to instill this basic idea in our boys.

If you can teach your son that negative actions have negative consequences while he's small, you are equipping him to succeed in the real world when he's older.

A mama who routinely overlooks her son's disobedience for his first five years will be at a severe disadvantage when kindergarten rolls around. A mama who tirelessly requires obedience and faithfully enforces consequences for disobedience for his first five years? Her boy will have infinitely less trouble listening to his teacher and respecting his classmates. Both boys may naturally have hearts prone to disobey, wanting to bypass mom's authority. But one will have been trained, and the other will not have been. The well-trained boy will be better positioned to succeed in school, relationships, and the workplace.

AN OVERLOOKED PREDICTOR OF FUTURE SUCCESS

Guess which of these factors is the strongest predictor of good grades for eighth-graders:

  a.) IQ
  b.) self-control

If you chose self-control, you would be correct.[2] And the impact of exercising self-control goes well beyond good grades. Studies show that self-control measured in childhood is a strong predictor of a child's success and well-being in adulthood.[3]

If your first-grader is currently in the room adjacent to you, running around with a lampshade on his head while chugging a soda he fished out of the trash can—and if you just read that last paragraph and freaked out so hard that your heart dropped into your butt— stick with me. This is actually good news for moms.

Why is this information massively encouraging? Because self-control is something we can teach! And we can start working on it while our boys are still in diapers. There is so much room for learning and growth here, and we are just the right ladies for the job. So buck up!

Self-control is both critically important *and* requires a seemingly infinite amount of training and effort to establish. Yes, I know, small boys are basically poster children for impulsivity. If there seems a chasm between your miniature Jersey Shore cast member and the man of God you hope to raise, TAKE HEART. Also, take inventory of your son's self-control baseline. It takes years to see the fruit of your work in this area. Mark the beginning so you can more fully enjoy the progress later. How do you establish this elusive but important self-control?

NATURAL CONSEQUENCES = THE FOUNDATION OF SELF-CONTROL

The more often your son experiences that acting a fool will cost him something, the less he will act a fool. Little Sherwin Williams

McFingerpaint acted on his impulses repeatedly—until the cost of his foolishness was too high. Allowing natural consequences conveys cost in a tangible way, even while our boys are toddlers. Counting the cost requires our sons to think beyond their impulses. Doing this repeatedly, every day, even in the seemingly small situations, builds self-control.

See, you're probably already doing this! Keep going. This will require resolve and some stress on your part. It will certainly involve some screaming and tantrums on his part. Do it anyway.

If you told three-year-old Charlemagne that throwing his food will get him an immediate trip to napville, calmly and firmly allow that consequence to play out.

You said finishing dinner was the prerequisite to the brownie, but Amadeus chose not to eat. Don't you dare bend when his eyes well up and his long lashes are grazing his brows. Even if he looks cuter than a golden retriever puppy. Don't you do it. When he busts out that pouty lip, you raise him a wide-eyed reminder of his own choices.

If six-year-old Geraldo tells you no when you remind him to put his toys away? Straight to jail. (Whoa. I meant the toys—I'm not Kim Jong Un.) Like a little laundry basket toy jail that he'll need to do chores to get them out of later.

BEYOND EARLY BEDTIMES AND MISSED TREATS: PRACTICALLY TEACHING SELF-CONTROL THROUGH NATURAL CONSEQUENCES

How about some ideas for imparting these concepts to our little boys that are more pleasant?

Story is your BFF. A good story is powerful, entertaining, and sticks around in the brain longer than a rule. Plus, it's always easier to see someone else's speck than it is to notice our own plank. Use story to help your boys see how the world works, and how consequences unfold for others. Here are a few of our favorites.

Books to teach natural consequences and self-control:

> It's always easier to see someone else's speck
> than it is to notice our own plank. Use story
> to help your boys see how the world works,
> and how consequences unfold for others.

What Should Danny Do? THE POWER TO CHOOSE SERIES. Danny is a boy making choices. This is a choose-your-own-adventure picture book. You can read it over and over, and it's a different story each time, depending on what your son chooses for Danny. Sometimes he has the option to choose a bad attitude. Your son will see how that works out for him.

Inch by Inch by Leo Lionni

The Gardener by Sarah Stewart

Halfway Herbert by Francis Chan

The Boy Who Cried Wolf by Aesop

One mom shared that her young son lied frequently. She told him Aesop's story of the shepherd boy, and it resonated with her son. This one is so easy to share while driving or on a walk, or in a conversation at the end of a disciplinary conversation.

Ask your son to find good examples of self-control or of natural consequences coming to bear in shows, movies, or books.

Or if you see a character reaping the consequences of bad decisions, pause the movie and ask your son what he noticed.

WHAT TO SAY ABOUT THOSE NATURAL CONSEQUENCES

If you've told your son about the consequence for shirking your authority, and he does it anyway, feel free to let the consequence speak for itself. This helps you to stay calm, knowing that you're obeying God in your calling to train up your child in the way he should go.

As your son grows a little older and can understand longer explanations, give him a little more understanding. For me, that usually looks something like this:

Me: I told you to bring your library book in the house, but you left it outside anyway. What happened to it?

Son: The rain ruined it.

Me: Such a bummer. That book costs twenty dollars. How are you going to pay the library back for that?

Son: I have ten dollars.

Me: Sounds like you'll need to come up with ten more dollars. I have some chores available for hire. But that's a lot of money, so it will require a lot of work.

Son: I don't want to spend my money on that! And I don't want to do chores.

Me: (Genuinely) I don't blame you. I know you were saving up.

Son: This stinks! This is unfair!

Me: What's unfair is that you borrowed a book and ruined it because you didn't follow instructions. In order to make it right, you need to replace it. I understand you're upset about that, but this was the choice you made.

Warning: Doing this will be more work for you—but only in the short term. In the long run, you're raising sons who are learning responsibility and self-control through your willingness to bear with them. Good job, Mama!

BIBLE VERSES TO INSTILL THE CONCEPT OF NATURAL CONSEQUENCES AND SELF-CONTROL

Below are a few verses you can read to your son when you explain why you're holding him accountable for his decisions.

> For he who has done wrong will receive the consequences of the wrong which he has done.
>
> Colossians 3:25 NASB

No discipline seems pleasant at the time, but painful. Later on, however, it produces a harvest of righteousness and peace for those who have been trained by it.

Hebrews 12:11

All of you must obey those who rule over you. There are no authorities except the ones God has chosen. Those who now rule have been chosen by God. So whoever opposes the authorities opposes leaders whom God has appointed. Those who do that will be judged. If you do what is right, you won't need to be afraid of your rulers. But watch out if you do what is wrong! You don't want to be afraid of those in authority, do you? Then do what is right, and you will be praised. The one in authority serves God for your good. But if you do wrong, watch out! Rulers don't carry a sword for no reason at all. They serve God. And God is carrying out his anger through them. The ruler punishes anyone who does wrong. You must obey the authorities. Then you will not be punished. You must also obey them because you know it is right.

Romans 13:1–5 NIrV

The rod and reproof give wisdom,
    but a child left to himself brings shame to his mother.

Proverbs 29:15 ESV

The LORD became angry with Solomon. That's because his heart had turned away from the LORD, the God of Israel. He had appeared to Solomon twice. He had commanded Solomon not to worship other gods. But Solomon didn't obey the LORD. So the LORD said to Solomon, "You have chosen not to keep my covenant. You have decided not to obey my rules. I commanded you to do what I told you. But you did not do it. So you can be absolutely sure I will tear the kingdom away from you. I will give it to one of your officials."

1 King 11:9–11 NIrV

WAITING

YOUR CALL IS IMPORTANT TO US.
PLEASE CONTINUE TO NOT WHINE LIKE A TWO-YEAR-OLD

> He that has patience may compass anything.
>
> —François Rabelais,
> *Gargantua and Pantagruel*

> But if we hope for what we do not yet have, we **wait** for it patiently.
>
> —Romans 8:25, emphasis added

Paul's words in Romans are a lofty goal for us here in the twenty-first century. Nowadays, instead of waiting patiently, we numb out on our iPhones.

At the risk of sounding like a crochety old hag, I must say that kids today do not know how to wait. They don't. *Because we don't require them to.* Instead, we hand them a screen. Waiting is a lost art, and one that is utterly fundamental to the Christian life.

In one study, 95 percent of people said that patience is a virtue. The same respondents reported that they grew frustrated after:

- 16 seconds of waiting for a website to load
- 25 seconds of waiting for a traffic light to change
- 18 seconds of looking for a pen

Three-quarters of the respondents said they believe the decline in patience is due to on-demand digital technology.[1]

PATIENCE AND PARENTING

"When I was a kid, they hadn't invented the internet, or 'streaming' shows," I told my kids, who were all born well after the last VHS tape had been buried in a time capsule. "We had to wait a whole week for a new episode of *The Fresh Prince of Bel-Air*."

"WOW! Tell us another story of the ancient times, Mother!"

"During the magical thirty minutes of Will Smith jokes that would get anyone canceled today, you'd experience a thing called 'commercial breaks.' If you were alive back then, you'd strategically plan bathroom breaks and snack refills around these pockets of time. Not only that, but if you were with your mom at the grocery store, you'd need to respectfully ask her to hurry home so you could catch your show. If you missed it, it was gone. No way to watch it on demand."

"Whoa, Mom . . . how old are you again?"

I should've told them about request lines, when we picked up an actual phone with a dial tone, waiting on hold with a radio station for an hour just to request "MMMBop." (Which, btw, you should definitely introduce to your kids if you haven't yet, because it totally holds up.)

Gone are the days of waiting. We're living in the most convenient of times. I drive a car. I have air conditioning. My car has air conditioning! I can look up any fact from a rectangle I keep in my pocket. I can listen to any song I want, anytime. Music, TV, even groceries are summoned by us, and delivered to us, almost immediately. Waiting is like, so passé.

The only problem? Learning to wait is critical to developing patience and an understanding that we are not the center of the universe.

Our culture champions self. Self-service, self-satisfaction, self-glorification.

As people of faith, and specifically moms of faith, we are stewards of a different mindset. We champion serving others, seeking the welfare of our neighbors, and glorifying God. In fact, Tim Keller aptly captured this mindset as "self-forgetfulness," and he urged Christians to embrace the freedom we enjoy when we pursue lives built not on self, but on serving God and serving others.[2] If our lives are God-oriented, you'd better believe we'll be spending a lot of time waiting.

So how do we proceed? We want to train and raise little ones to be like David, who the Bible describes as a man after God's own heart.[3] We live in a culture that requires less of our boys than ever. We refuse to go along with the status quo, thankyouverymuch. We are mama bears. We are stewards of time, talents, and fruit snacks, and we refuse to allow the culture to erode our boys' characters. Prepare for battle, girls.

"Hard times create strong men. Strong men create good times. Good times create weak men. And, weak men create hard times."[4]

Is it just me, or does this quote from G. Michael Hopf's novel *Those Who Remain* seem to prophesy hard times ahead?

We don't need to stress. But we do want to be aware of the ways our culture is undermining the good we are prayerfully working to instill. We acknowledge first that our son's outward behavior isn't our primary goal in developing patience in his heart. Rather, our primary goal for our sons is that they become men who eagerly await the return of Jesus, who are deeply invested in building the kingdom of God, whose priorities align with the very Spirit of God. We also

> Our primary goal for our sons is that they become men who eagerly await the return of Jesus, who are deeply invested in building the kingdom of God, whose priorities align with the very Spirit of God.

acknowledge the reality that the mom reading this may have just received a phone call from the principal about her first-grade son who tattooed a girl's name on his leg with Sharpie, blamed another student, and then punched his brother. Did I say the mom reading this? I meant the mom *writing this*. (You'd better believe this child experienced some natural consequences after that doozy of a day.)

My pastor says that God likes to stack the deck against himself. We look at impossibly bleak situations, and we cannot see a way out. We can't see how this poop diaper of a behavioral problem could possibly resolve into something beautiful. But that's the fun part of following Jesus. Not during the poop-diaper situation, perhaps. But on the other side of it, we look back at the before picture and say, "Wow, the only reason little Pippin changed was God. God moved mountains in that little heart. Glory to God." And we see yet again that God is incredible. Because He is currently parenting *us*, teaching us to wait on Him, developing our own patience. He will efficiently accomplish all this as we train up, bear with, and fight for the hearts of our little wild banshee boys.

So if you're working with a little man whose patience quotient is lacking, you take heart, mama. You are in great company. As a mom of many kids, with patience baselines all over the map, I can assure you that God will meet you exactly where you are, as you come alongside your little guy—wherever he is. And God will give you exactly what you need to grow him.

Let's roll up those sleeves today and look for opportunities to train up our boys to wait well, that they would become men who don't administer their own tattoos or punch their bro for taking too long in the bathroom.

TOOLS FOR GROWING THEIR PATIENCE MUSCLES

Narrate your own waiting, both the good examples and the bad. Provide context and the tools you're using to not flip your lid.

"Wow, that mom up there is using the school drop-off line as a parking space again. I'm frustrated while I wait for her to get out of her car and walk her child to the classroom while blocking the entire line. But I'm going to take a deep breath and remember that Jesus died for her sins too." (After a moment of silence) "Lord, will you please give me patience? I'm struggling."

Encourage your son to save up for a toy or pet he wants. Saving money requires long-term patience, and repetitive waiting every time he wants to buy something lesser in the short term. If you take a trip to the toy store for a birthday present but your son wants to buy a toy for himself, ask if he has any birthday money saved up, or if he would like to earn some by doing chores around the house. Start small! Like, under five dollars. This is a great way to practice delaying gratification.

Play a board game. Taking turns is an excellent way to practice waiting. If your kids are anything like mine, they will find this difficult! But repetition is your friend. Remind your little guy that waiting is part of life, and that practice will make him stronger. Don't be surprised if he doesn't receive that observation with glee. Trust that every little deposit of truth and wisdom is building his patience.

Mark a calendar and count down to fun events. Christmas, Thanksgiving, Halloween, a trip to visit relatives. A simple Advent calendar is perfect for this. Talk about your excitement and also about how it's hard to wait, but what a thrill when the day arrives. You could let him mark each day off the calendar, or make a paper chain like we did in the olden days.

Share biblical examples of people who had to wait. Talk about people who waited well, and people who didn't wait so well. What were the consequences of their impatience? Example: Esau gave up a double share of his inheritance for Jacob's bowl of SpaghettiOs and a hot cross bun. Why? Because he came home hungry and couldn't wait a few minutes to cook up his own dino nuggets. Esau's inability to wait led him to make a very bad choice that he would regret for the rest of his life.[5]

Another example: God wanted to lead the Israelites into the land He promised them. But the people grew whiny and impatient, and as a consequence, almost every Israelite who left Egypt didn't get to see the Promised Land. Their kids did, though. There are consequences when people don't obey God. But God is still patient with us! He is always waiting there for us to turn away from our sins and turn back to trusting Him.

Notice and talk out your son's patience, or lack thereof. Look for moments of his day that require patience and you will find a zillion. Share what you see with your little dude. "I saw you wait patiently for the boy at the playground to go down the slide so you could take a turn. Great job, buddy." Or maybe it's, "Hey, man, I noticed you were screaming like a train and stomping like an Irish Riverdancer waiting your turn for the drinking fountain. Any ideas for how you can wait more patiently next time?" (Owning your own impatience, or victories in waiting, will give you credibility here.)

Most of all, be encouraged, oh undercaffeinated one! The tantrum your son just threw—when met with your calm reminder of truth—is strengthening his character. Keep going. Every time you tell that little wild child that he must wait for dessert, wait for Christmas to open the present, or wait until mom has had her coffee to bust out the moon sand—you are requiring his little heart to flex his patience muscle. Good job, mom!

BIBLE VERSES YOU CAN MEMORIZE TOGETHER TO DEVELOP PATIENCE

> Wait for the LORD;
>   be strong and take heart
>   and wait for the LORD.
>
>   Psalm 27:14

In the morning, LORD, you hear my voice;
    in the morning I lay my requests before you
    and wait expectantly.

Psalm 5:3

I **wait** for the LORD, my whole being **wait**s,
    and in his word I put my hope.

Psalm 130:5, emphasis added

Be patient, then, brothers and sisters, until the Lord's coming. See how the farmer waits for the land to yield its valuable crop, patiently waiting for the autumn and spring rains.

James 5:7

#4

FUN

The world: "My son is a grump when he has to do any task he doesn't like, especially chores. That's just the way he is. He can do chores when he's older. While he is young, he should only focus on the things he enjoys, and on his schoolwork."

Mission-minded boy mom: "Fun is the seasoning of everyday life. And chores are part of stewardship and serving others, so I'll train my son in diligence and responsibility—seasoned with fun—starting when he is small."

Helping your son have a pleasant disposition will serve him the rest of his life. One important way to do this is by infusing fun into your days. There is science to support the healing effects of laughter. Show your boy that appropriate fun, humor, and levity are accessible all around him—even in the mundane and difficult. We will explore the benefits of infusing fun into his life, and ideas for adding humor, in the next two chapters.

HUMOR

A GUY WALKS INTO A BAR . . . OUCH

A cheerful heart is good medicine,
but a broken spirit saps a person's strength.
—Proverbs 17:22 NLT

A person without a sense of humor is like a wagon without springs.
It's jolted by every pebble on the road.

—Attributed to Henry Ward Beecher

If you think that a sense of humor can't possibly be as important for moms to impart as some of these other chapters, hear me out for a minute.

Humor infuses an invisible, textural layer to the human experience. A life lived without humor would be like eating food without salt. Bakers add a pinch of salt to cookies because it creates a background or contrast to better experience the sweetness. Humor does this for everyday life.

If life were a decorated Christmas tree in a dark room, humor would be the tree lights. You see the entire picture, the messy beauty, in a way that you couldn't without them.

Humor brings pleasure, bliss, and family bonding during the good times. It is a glimmer of light, and a healthy replacement for worry, in the hard times.

Lest you write off my championing of humor as personal preference, (my dad was a comedy writer, so finding the funny runs in my blood), here are several scientific reasons you'll want to prioritize laughter and humor in the raising of your little humans. Turns out there's a bunch!

Did you know:

Laughter increases pain tolerance.

Genuine laughter decreases cortisol (stress hormone) levels.[1]

The body's response to laughter is physiologically similar to the body's response to exercise.

In one study, humor therapy was used to treat agitation in dementia patients. Humor treatment was as effective as antipsychotic drugs in reducing agitation, but without side effects.[2]

One psychologist writes that humor "dissects anxiety so it no longer has the power to paralyze" and "preserves a sense of mastery, hope, and integrity."[3] This empowers kids (and grown-ups!) to reframe the difficulties we all inevitably face.

Shared laughter deepens empathy and attachment.[4]

Laughter boosts the immune system, regulates blood pressure, and improves memory, focus, attention, and concentration.[5]

For our purposes, this next one is my favorite: Humor also strengthens relationship between students and teacher, which may help "draw out more introverted students."[6]

Humor will improve our relationships with our boys and help them remember what we say.

Moms! We are our boys' first and forever teacher. So this last little tidbit is important and helpful to us as we build our lifelong relationships with our baby hooligan-men. Humor will improve our relationships with our boys and help them remember what we say. (The Lord knows we need that.)

A TIMELESS BUFFER FOR AN ANXIOUS AND DEPRESSED GENERATION

The kids aren't alright. Unless you've been living under a rock, you've seen countless headlines over the last several years about the alarming decline in mental health among kids and teens. What's causing the problem? Much of the research points to both the increase of time spent online and the breakdown of families. I've mentioned this in previous chapters, and will continue to show you new research, because there are tangible ways parents can get in front of generational trends, if we are paying attention.

Initially, researchers suggested that girls growing up today are the primary sufferers of the digital media explosion. What about the boys? Boys who are heavy users of social media were twice as likely to be depressed as boys who did not use social media. Because girls who are heavy social media users are three times as likely to be depressed as nonusers, much of the conversation about the harmful effects on our kids centered around who was being harmed more.

But researchers are beginning to look more closely at the negative impacts on boys, and what they're finding is alarming. Depression rates in boys were up 161 percent in 2021 compared with 2010.[7] Suicide rates in boys ages ten to fourteen increased 111 percent in 2020, compared with 2009.[8] This data is gut-wrenching.

How did we get from a conversation about humor to depression data?

Because we need to take inventory of the climate our boys are being raised in. We need to appreciate the stakes so we can equip them with the tools they'll need to not get sucked into the vortex that's devouring the hearts and minds of too many boys. Since personal computers hit the scene in the 1970s, boys have been lured away from real life and drawn instead to the digital wonderland that's constantly beckoning them into solitary confinement. Before he even takes his first steps, a young boy today will be drawn to the soft, numbing ease of endless video programming. Soon he's tapping on the tablet, then on to gaming away every free moment. We want more for our boys. And that's going to involve doing things differently than swaths of moms have been doing for the last decade or two. We will need to pull our sons out of the digital dumpster, and then be their tour guides out here in the real world. If it sounds hard, that's because it is. Humor is going to get you both through it.

TEACHING HIM NOT TO TAKE HIMSELF TOO SERIOUSLY

The best way to help your son laugh at himself is to laugh at *yourself.* If you do something silly, share it! My mom was the best at this. She'd often confuse words, creating very awkward social situations. One time she was with a group of girlfriends touring a farm. She pointed to a large tractor and loudly asked the tour guide, "Is that a concubine?" (A concubine is basically a live-in mistress.) All the chatter in her tour group came to a halt as the tour guide raised his eyebrows and corrected her: "Did you mean to ask if it was a combine?" (A large harvesting machine.)

"Oh, yeah. Whatever. Is it a combine?" Mom said she laughed the whole ride home, and the story has gone into our family's history of awkward moments. Laughing at your own mistakes shows your son that it's okay to mess up, and that these moments can even provide good entertainment later.

A boy who can laugh off setbacks and embarrassment is a boy who is learning resilience.

TEACHING GOOD HUMOR

Long before your little man hits the literal and figurative stink of a junior high locker room, he will laugh at plenty of bodily function jokes.

Do not despair if his idea of funny is giving you flashbacks to Beavis and Butt-head. Observe and take mental note. We have so many jobs as moms, and one of them is to educate our boys' sense of humor.

Today's potty joker is tomorrow's clever humorist. But only with some help and instruction along the way. This is where we moms come in. We teach good humor by showing him the funny, *and* reminding him of our house culture. We laughed *a lot* in my house growing up. But if anyone mentioned a word that only belonged in the bathroom, they'd get the side-eye from Dad and be reminded to avoid "vulgarity." Whatever your house rules, remind your little dude. And keep showing him the funny. He'll get there.

HUMOR HELPS MOM TOO

Ladies, I cannot tell you how many times humor has saved me in the throes of hard, horrible parenting days. Like the time I had four kids under six, and my boys took turns breaking legs for a year. The orthopedist was like, "Yes, ma'am, despite the statistical improbabilities, your sons are on their third broken leg. Try not to get ranch dressing inside the cast like last time." I had one kid in a stroller, another in a baby carrier, and a third in a miniature wheelchair, chauffeured by my six-year-old daughter. We bumbled into a Mexican restaurant where we were meeting my dad for lunch. He took in the sight of us, eyes growing wide, and then he laughed. He apologized for laughing, but I stopped him to join in. This was insane! Our laughter brought me out of my desperation and into a zone of marveling about the ridiculousness. We shared nachos, we shared stories, and the helium effects of our shared laughter lifted me back onto my feet.

Working your tail off to raise little men intentionally is going to be the hardest work of your life. You'll be sweating and crying, so you better add some laughter in there, or else it's just not any fun at all.

Here is a practical idea for adding humor to the hard. Think of something funny that happened in your parenting today, yesterday, this week, whatever. Text a friend about it. Better yet, make it a voice text. Laughing with a fellow mom about hard parenting stuff is the surest way to lighten your load.

FUNNY BOOK RECOMMENDATIONS FOR KIDS

Two and up:
Bear Snores On by Karma Wilson

Not a Box by Antoinette Portis

Three and up:
Can I Be Your Dog? by Troy Cummings

Mac and Cheese by Sarah Weeks

Mother Bruce by Ryan T. Higgins

The Long Dog by Eric Seltzer

What About Worms by Ryan T. Higgins

Winnie-the-Pooh by A. A. Milne (the chapter book, as a read-aloud)

Four and up:
A Mother for Choco by Keiko Kasza

If I Built a House by Chris Van Duson

Stuart Little by E. B. White

The Gruffalo by Julia Donaldson

The Stinky Cheese Man and Other Fairly Stupid Tales by Jon Scieszka

Who Wet My Pants? by Bob Shea

For more funny book recommendations, check out my website, MollyDefrank.com.

TEDIOUS RESPONSIBILITIES

DO THE DISHES, CINDERELLY

Well begun is half done.

—Aristotle[1]

"Son, why aren't you cleaning your room?" This kid was a master chore-avoider. If he'd put half this effort into the chores themselves, he'd have been done an hour ago. I wasn't surprised to find him in the kitchen.

"I need a drink of water."

Ah, Rapid Onset Chore Thirst. Nothing incites thirst like bed-time or chore time. "We just ate lunch, and you drank plenty of water. You can drink all the water you want—after your room is clean."

"WHAT?! This is child abuse. You need to be reported."

I had to bite my lip to keep a straight face.

"Clean. The room." I said it slowly and deliberately.

He turned back to me and said, "You're right, Mom." And from that day forward, he cleaned his room like Marie Kondo herself.

Kidding! What actually followed was forty grueling minutes of his whining and my eye twitching.

Isn't motherhood fun?

How about this one. My teenage son, when prompted to make his bed, tried to argue that he purposefully left it unmade—for hygienic purposes.

"Mom. Sunlight kills bacteria, even through a window. My bed faces the window, and when I leave it unmade, my sheets are getting cleaner. So it's actually smarter to leave it unmade."

Nice try, son. "A for creativity. Now go make your bed."

Here's the point: It's our duty to lead our boys past chore resistance. This is how good habits are formed. In between that desperate scene and a fully grown, responsible adult man stands a mother who is willing to say, "No, sir, you may not wiggle your way out of your responsibilities." Because inevitably, life will include plenty of days that require you to push through responsibilities that you do not enjoy. The more our little dudes practice completing chores they hate, the better and more efficient they will become at it. Soon they will enjoy the satisfaction that comes from a job well done.

COMPELLING RESEARCH

A strong predictor of success in a person's mid-twenties is participation in chores at three and four years old.[2] This is magnificent news. That means that every time you require Gilbert to contribute to the household functioning, you're investing in his future. Every time you refuse to allow little Nero to protest his way out of work, you gird him up for the hard parts of life.

Or how about this one: A study of almost ten thousand elementary-aged children showed that kids who were required to do chores in kindergarten boasted clear advantages in third grade in "self-competence, prosocial behavior, and self-efficacy," and the kids who helped with household chores regularly also scored higher on self-reported measures of academic ability and life satisfaction.[3]

No one is as invested in your son's future success as you are. If you're not willing to stand firm against his ornery objections to chores, no one else will do it for you. Which means that no one will do it for him. This is an opportunity to cultivate and hone our own sense of grit! Because we all know how much easier it is in the short term to do the work ourselves. But training our boys is worth all our effort and headaches—in the long term.

A SIMPLE RESPONSIBILITY-BUILDER

Get him a pet. I know. I know pets add a little more complexity to life. But hear me out.

In a culture where everyone is turning inward, where on-demand means kids get what they want when they want it, pets are a cute, fluffy way to resist, flipping this trend on its head.

Don't tell my husband I'm saying this, but I'm secretly glad that he brought my sons to the pet shop and came home with a box of rats. Gross? Yes. But get this.

My older sons are eleven and thirteen as I write this, and they are required on a regular basis to stop what they are doing and check on their creatures. Weekly, they negotiate how to clean the cage. They are forced to respond to the needs of a being outside of themselves. Does the care of tiny, creepy rodents sometimes entail griping and attempts to get out of work? You betcha. But I will never forget when my work-avoidant boy finally finished his pet responsibilities and said, "You know what? It's actually not as hard as I thought it would be to clean the cage. And it feels satisfying to have a clean place for them." Plus, now their bedroom doesn't smell like a foot.

That lightbulb moment was invaluable. Every time your boy pushes through important work he doesn't want to do, but must

> Every time your boy pushes through important
> work he doesn't want to do, but must do anyway,
> he is learning a valuable skill for his life.

do anyway, he is learning a valuable skill for his life. Pets bring both fun and work. They show him that the two are not mutually exclusive, and that, in fact, work and fun often come as a pair if you choose the right attitude!

You could also try a fish. But they are considerably less hardy, and in our experience, they die off quickly, despite best efforts. Outdoor cats make for very low-maintenance pets. Dogs are a ton of work, so I'd get his full buy-in on the front end before getting one. But there's no pet quite like a dog to get your boy off his heinie and into responsibility mode: walking, feeding, cleaning up after.

INFUSING FUN AND MEANING INTO THE MENIAL

Work was part of life even before sin entered the world, when everything was perfect. It's important to provide context for our sons' work, and to help them find value in their smallest responsibilities.

Modeling a joy-filled attitude as we tackle our own responsibilities will go a long way in teaching our sons. I am a work in progress on this front, to be sure. Share with your boys how you deal with jobs you don't want to do. Most of all, remember that the process is long and takes time. Training requires repetition.

As mom, you have the fun job of helping identify which tasks/chores your son is better at or more drawn to completing. Does it really matter that Gilligan doesn't like cleaning his room? No, no it doesn't. He still has to do it. But you may identify specific chores that he's more uniquely drawn to: cooking, pet care, building a new kitchen stool. If you have the option to assign him tasks that he was wired to do, then by all means, help him hone those.

CHORES YOUR SON CAN HELP WITH BY AGE

TODDLERS

Even before our little dudes are mobile, they can put toys back in a basket. Would it be easier and faster to just do it yourself? Yes. But take this opportunity to help him begin to understand that life is play and work.

TWO–FIVE

Empty the dishwasher. Move dishes to lower cupboards if you need to.

Feed the dog (with assistance). Scoop the kibble; place the bowl on Fido's mat.

Put clothes away in drawers.

Sort laundry.

SIX–TEN

Take the dog for a walk.

Scoop the dog mess in the yard.

Vacuum the vehicle at the self-service car wash.

Unload/put away groceries.

Dishwasher helper.

Wipe bathroom counters.

Clean glass slider doors/windows/mirrors.

Sweep.

Remove trash/items left in car backseat.

10+

Chores listed above and . . .

Learn how to do his laundry—loading into the washer, moving to the dryer.

Fold and hang his clothes.

Cook an easy dinner.

IDEAS TO HELP MAKE THE CHORES FUN

Lead with a great attitude. If you're wearing a smile, they are more likely to.

Blast fun music. My youngest kids loved the cleanup song, but any favorite upbeat tune will do.

Pretend you're a team of super spies, dismantling enemy devices (stray socks) by throwing them in the victory bucket (hamper). Set a timer for five minutes. Can you defeat the aliens before the timer dings? (My oldest invented this game to help her siblings clean. It works every time.)

BIBLE VERSES TO REMIND US OF THE IMPORTANCE OF HARD WORK

All hard work pays off.
But if all you do is talk, you will be poor.

Proverbs 14:23 NIrV

Work at everything you do with all your heart. Work as if you were working for the Lord, not for human masters.

Colossians 3:23 NIrV

You people who don't want to work, think about the ant!
Consider its ways and be wise!
It has no commander.
It has no leader or ruler.
But it stores up its food in summer.
It gathers its food at harvest time.

Proverbs 6:6–8 NIrV

#5

BRAVERY

The world: "Because our value changes depending on our achievements, failure is especially debilitating. Better not take too many risks."

Mission-minded boy mom: "In Christ, our value never wavers. I'll teach my son that failure needn't debilitate him, *and* that God will use it for good. This empowers him to take the risks that he needs to for growth."

Many boys today are opting out of situations that require bravery, because they're trying to avoid anxiety: participating in class, initiating new friendships, trying out for a team. But our kids need to experience risks and failure in order to develop grit. Yes, this involves discomfort. But it also grows our sons' bravery muscles. As one Harvard psychologist put it, "Paradoxically, the best way to support anxious kids is often by encouraging them to get more comfortable with being uncomfortable."[1] Let's talk about how to do this practically, and why the exposure to risk actually helps our sons grow in courage.

13

FAILURE

PRACTICE MAKES PERFECT OPPORTUNITIES FOR MAKING MISTAKES

Failure is success in progress.

—Albert Einstein

He wanted the lead role in the play so badly, he could taste it. Perhaps I'm biased, but I was confident he had a good shot. The day came, the cast list was posted. I drove through the school pickup line, spotting my little thespian. He opened the car door and held it together until he closed it behind him.

My little man shot for the stars, hoping for Simba. He wound up Hyena #3.

To say he was devastated is an understatement. My heart ached alongside his. Disappointment is tough. We sat in the sad for a little while. Then I tried to encourage him.

"Listen. I'm amazed at what you can do up there. You're good at this. And today you felt the sting of not getting picked. It sure does hurt, huh? I'm so sorry. Can I tell you what encourages me when I don't get picked? There's a verse in the Bible that tells us that God works all things out for His glory, and for the good of those who love Him. He will take the stuff that seems terrible—and here's where it gets amazing—He turns it around and uses it for good! Even when we can't see it. Now, I have no idea how or why this is better than what you and I both wanted, but I trust God that it's true."

"But, WHY? Why and how could this possibly be better? I worked so hard."

"I have no idea, bud. Because I can't see the whole picture. But you have two choices. You can quit. And you'll probably never get another chance to try out if you do that, because you can't quit once you get cast. Or, you can show up and be the best Hyena #3 that stage has ever seen. You can learn and grow and try out for the next play. And if you don't get picked for the part you want then, you'll keep going, keep working, keep learning."

"This is the worst day ever."

I thought my speech was pretty decent, but bro rejected it like a brown banana. I talked it through some more. I listened, I sat. I made him a sugary snack I'd never have allowed under better circumstances. And you know what, after a few *hours* of this—I needed to TAP OUT. I started wishing he'd been cast just so I did not have to repeat the same common-sense motivational speech that felt like straight-up pearls before swine. (Cute swine.) Isn't motherhood so refining?

Here's the deal. Our boys need to experience failure. We all know failure's important because it develops perseverance, hard work, grit. (More on that later.) But for the believing mom, I think there's something even more fundamental that our boys' failures can teach—if we help facilitate.

Here it is: For the Christian, no matter how far you miss the mark, fail, don't achieve—your identity never changes. Nothing of critical importance breaks when you totally blow it or when you

> When we face failure, it stings. But Jesus is eternal, and our status in Him *will never change*. This is the most fundamental piece of hope we get to serve up for our boys.

don't get picked. Our earthly dreams for achievement are important, but they're nothing compared with the eternal hope that anchors our souls. When we face failure, it stings. But Jesus is eternal, and our status in Him *will never change*.

This is the most fundamental piece of hope we get to serve up for our boys while they're under our roof. We get to provide context for their failures or perceived failures. As your son grows in character and maturity, he will, hopefully, learn to assess his character and sin in a healthy and humble way. When he's small, he will likely be more focused on achievement failures than character failures. You'll keep teaching him. But the way he processes achievement failures will inform how he processes sin failures too! God is efficient with the seeds we plant.

Your son's exposure to failure with mom nearby is critical.

Because you're waiting right there to scoop him up, reminding him that he's still the apple of your eye and that his identity, his value, your love for him—none of it changes no matter his role in the play, his batting average, his GPA.

This is a critical foundational nugget of truth we want to chisel into his heart.

As your son grows into a man, what a gift for him to understand that his failures do not define him. Familiarize him with an eternal context for things not going his way. Assure him that God will work this steamy pile of mess out too. Your son will flex that muscle as he grows. And when he's fully grown, that man will have practiced contextualizing his failures against eternity. You're girding up his heart when life's inevitable setbacks come: a layoff, rejection from a girlfriend.

FAILURE AS A SPRINGBOARD FOR GROWTH

Now let's talk about how we can use failure as a playground for development. This is the fun part.

Failure as fun?! YES! Here are a few examples of famously successful people who overcame failure. What seems to separate the greats from the average people is their refusal to call it quits after hitting a wall. Share these examples with your boys, if they're big enough to understand.

Did you know . . .

- Martin Luther King Jr. got a C in public speaking during his first year of seminary. No joke. King went from merely passing public speaking to class valedictorian, and eventually delivering the most memorable speech of the century.[1]
- Michael Jordan didn't make the varsity basketball team his sophomore year of high school.
- The University of Southern California's film school rejected Steven Spielberg—three times. Years later, the school would award him an honorary degree.[2]
- Apple fired Steve Jobs from his own company. After founding two new companies, one of which was acquired by Apple, Jobs went on to launch the iPod and iPhone. "I didn't see it then, but it turned out that getting fired from Apple was the best thing that could have ever happened to me," he said in a Stanford commencement address.[3]

As moms who can see the big picture, we know that another strikeout does not define our son's entire baseball experience. Since we have a few more years under our belts, we need to share that perspective with our little dude. He can't see it yet. Tell him about the greats and their own setbacks along the way.

WHAT MOM CAN SAY TO HELP HIM PROCESS

Okay, so how do we help our boys to process failure? Whether it's a falling Lego tower or another strikeout at the plate, here are some specific things you can say to help him develop perspective in failure that will help him as he grows.

ACKNOWLEDGE HIS DISAPPOINTMENT.

"I can understand why you're frustrated."

"I know how hard you worked for it."

"I can see how much time you've put into this."

"It's okay to take a break."

"Do you want to talk about it?"

ASK WHAT HE IS HOPING TO ACCOMPLISH.

"Do you have a goal for how tall you are trying to make this tower?"

"Do you have a specific goal for your batting average/reading points/history grade this semester?"

"Do you have a plan for how to reach that goal?"

"Do you want help making a plan?"

CHEER HIM ON!

"I believe in you."

"You can do this."

"Keep going."

"Hard work beats talent any day."

"The attention you're giving to this is going to pay off."

Tell him where you've seen improvement. Note when those gains wouldn't have been possible without the failure! It'll help him connect the dots for the next endeavor.

Most important of all, keep reminding him of his inherent, un-wavering value as a child of God, despite any failure. (Remember, it will almost always appear that he doesn't care or doesn't receive that truth. Say it anyway. Plant the seeds. Your words will become his inner voice.)

RISK

RIDE THE SKATEBOARD! JUMP FROM THE HIGH DIVE! TRY OUT FOR THE TEAM!

> We are overprotecting our kids in the real world while underprotecting them online.
>
> —Jonathan Haidt, *The Anxious Generation*[1]

What if I told you that the healthiest way for your active boy to learn is by taking risks?

When Millard shoves a handful of dirt in his mouth, he learns that taste isn't a great sensory option for nonfood objects.

When Reginald jumps from the swing, he might learn that he's capable of negotiating cool tricks, or he might learn what the inside of an emergency room looks like.

When Bruce knocks on the neighbor's door for a playdate, he might learn how to make a new pal, or he might learn that he can survive rejection.

Risk is the teacher that has grown capable, strong, social boys since the beginning of time. Status-quo motherhood today is to overprotect and over-orchestrate for our boys—even in their play. Research shows that what our young boys need is plenty of unstructured time to learn how the world works—by doing. We seem to collectively have bought into a lie that if we protect our son just so, choosing the exact right diaper brand, and prohibiting nonorganic produce, he will never get hurt. Unfortunately, despite our best efforts in life, our son will at some point get hurt, fall, and fail. We want to help him learn how to get back up after he does fall and get hurt, and what it means when a risk doesn't pay off. The only way to teach him that is by allowing him to take risks.

Here is where mission-minded mamas can actually breathe a sigh of relief. Cultural, overprogrammed motherhood spikes motherly anxiety and is counterproductive. Allowing our little dudes to play, explore, try new things—without our overinvolvement—does more for his confidence, psyche, and even his social life than any of our lectures or lessons could. Huzzah!

PHYSICAL BENEFITS OF RISK-TAKING

> For physical development they need physical play and physical risk taking. Virtual battles in a video game confer little or no physical benefit.[2]

Scrapes, bruises, trips to urgent care—all this is part of the boy-mom gig. Research tells us that boys' play is generally riskier than girls' is. Mamas already knew this.

But something odd has happened to this current generation of little boys. They're avoiding the risky play that boys have always needed for healthy development. Why? Because parents are scared to let little Johnny risk a scraped knee or bruised arm.

The research shows us that jumping, falling, and getting back up again is beneficial for our boys. Not only is it good, it is necessary!

> In the age of overplanned, hyper-Pinterestified
> kid activities, take solace in knowing that rejecting
> the status quo of helicoptering is actually
> easier for mom, and better for your son.

Your son learns that he can take on a new challenge, even when the butterflies in his stomach tempt him to avoid it. Every time your son tackles a new goal or obstacle, he learns, adapts, grows. In the age of overplanned, hyper-Pinterestified kid activities, take solace in knowing that rejecting the status quo of helicoptering is actually *easier* for mom, and better for your son. Not only that, but risks also teach him how to build relationships, which can buffer future mental health problems.

SOCIAL RISKS PREPARE HIM FOR RELATIONSHIPS, WHICH PROTECT HIM FROM LONELINESS

Taking social risks like asking the neighbor to play, telling a joke, or phoning a friend—these initiatives build confidence and understanding in the hearts of our sons. Social risk-taking builds socially aware boys. If Billy tries to bite his friend at preschool, he soon will learn that no one wants to sit near him at snack time. He took a risk, learned the natural consequence of biting his friend (maybe he got a bite back?), and hopefully decided that the consequence was not worth his action. He also learns the benefits of living out Jesus's golden rule (treat others the way you want to be treated) in the real world.

> For social development they need to learn the art of friendship, which is embodied; friends do things together, and as children they touch, hug, and wrestle. Mistakes are low cost, and can be rectified in real time. Moreover, there are clear embodied signals of this rectification, such as an apology with an appropriate facial expression.

A smile, a pat on the back or a handshake shows everyone that it's okay, both parties are ready to move on and continue playing, both are developing their skills of relationship repair. In contrast, as young people move their social relationships online, those relationships become disembodied, asynchronous, and sometimes disposable.[3]

Allowing your son to play, conflict, and work it out in the real world is giving him a gift. You're helping him acquire and use tools for social awareness, which is the key to building and maintaining strong relationships for the rest of his life.

In fact, if you'll allow me to cite more research about future happiness and success, Harvard conducted a study to find out what the best predictor of human happiness and longevity was. Do you know what they found, after studying hundreds of men across all incomes and ethnicities, for eighty years? The key to longevity, health, and happiness was not diet, income, or exercise. It was quality of relationships.[4] You help your boy develop this when you create space for him to interact with a friend, on his own terms. Can you believe how much your boy can gain from your simply texting a friend to meet at the park and drink coffee together on the bench while your boys . . . play? Incredible. (I know these playdates are often fraught with their own challenges: baby diaper blowouts, your toddler storming other people's picnics while you nurse an infant . . . I know, my friend. This season will pass. I promise that you will look back on the mayhem and smile. And in the meantime, know you're building skills in your boy, even if all you see are more grass stains and ripped knees.)

Yes, the studies I've cited have examined different angles, with slightly different findings as to the genesis of success and happiness. We can conclude that it's beneficial to cultivate all these things in our sons, including self-control and positive relationships. Also, isn't it interesting how "modern studies" continue to support the idea that life is best lived under God's design? With self-control, and connected in community.

HELP YOUR BOY ROOT DEEPLY, LET HIM PLAY FREELY

We are fooling ourselves to think that a five-year-old boy with headphones and tablet is "safer" than his five-year-old classmate who is jumping from the play structure.

Jonathan Haidt is a social psychologist and researcher at New York University as well as a *New York Times* bestselling author. In his book *The Anxious Generation*, he breaks down the massive cultural shift in our parenting over the last fifty years and explains why overprotecting our kids from real-life risky play is harmful, using the analogy of a failed experiment. In the 1980s, scientists set out to create self-sustaining life for eight people in a fully contained biosphere in Arizona. The food, water, and oxygen consumed were to be created and used within the sphere. The experiment failed quickly. The trees planted in the biosphere grew initially but fell over before they reached full maturity. Why? Because trees need to be blown by the wind while they are young to develop "stress wood to strengthen its roots and structure."[5] The wind presses against the trees, signaling to the root system to grow, expand, and anchor downward. Trees need adversity to develop strong roots.[6]

In the same way, human beings need difficulty and struggle to learn and grow.

When we prevent our young boys from the risky play they need, they won't develop the skills they need to navigate bigger risks that life inevitably will present.

> Well-intentioned parents who try to raise their children in a bubble of satisfaction, protected from frustration, consequences, and negative emotions, may be harming their children. They may be blocking the development of competence, self-control, frustration tolerance, and emotional self-management. Several studies find that such "coddling" or "helicopter parenting" is correlated with later anxiety disorders, low self-efficacy (which is the inner confidence that one can do what is needed to reach one's goals), and difficulty adjusting to college.[7]

KEEP IT SIMPLE, AND PRAY!

One reason moms feel tremendous anxiety allowing their sons to take risks is because we falsely assume that we can control their health and well-being at all times. That's simply not the case. Remember that God loves your son more than you do. Yes, you are called to reasonably protect him, but you are also called to train him up, and that training involves his own risks and failures. We do not control every movement, bump, and bruise. So take the pressure off yourself, and lift your fears to the Lord. Pray for his heart and mind to grow in wisdom and understanding, as he learns and grows from the risks he takes under your loving care. Those risks are a chance for him to grow, *and* for mom to grow, by leaning on God in prayer.

I'll never forget the first time I allowed my nine-year-old son to walk a quarter mile to our mailbox alone to get the mail. Every minute he was gone felt like an hour. My heart pounded, and I realized, "Oh my gosh, this is just a glimpse of my future as my kids grow older and more independent. Is this only a taste of him moving away to college!?" I've experienced the same longings and fear sending them to summer camp, or on a beach trip with a friend when I wasn't there to supervise. This helpless longing is an opportunity for our hearts to abide in the powerful God who always sees our sons and is always able to guide and protect these boys—infinitely better than we can. Lift your heart to Him! *"Lord, please multiply my boy's common sense. Please keep him safe. Please remind him of who he is in you. Please convict him of sin if he is drawn toward it. Please calm my heart. Thank you that you control all things."*

GRIT

BUILD AN EXPENSIVE, NONFUNCTIONING ROCKET

As much as talent counts, effort counts twice.

—Angela Duckworth, *Grit*

In 2006, Elon Musk attempted to create a reusable rocket that could return home after being launched into space. He invested $100 million of his own money in the project. The funding would cover three attempted rocket launches. The first attempt failed. The second attempt also failed. The third attempt: failure again. He was nearly bankrupt, but instead of calling it quits, this man audaciously invested more money—just enough for one more launch. On the brink of shutdown, the fourth rocket succeeded.

Angela Duckworth, famed author and researcher of the bestselling book *Grit*, defines the word as "the tendency to sustain interest in and effort toward very long-term goals."[1] Certainly, there are many brilliant rocket scientists. But an abnormally giant grit quotient separated Musk from the rest. (The hundreds of millions of dollars probably also played a role. But again, grit undoubtedly fueled Musk's ability to earn that quantity of cash.) We non-Muskian mamas may not have hundreds of millions of dollars, but we all can cultivate grit in our boys. Research says boys today desperately need it.

According to the *Wall Street Journal*, boys have lost motivation in school in recent years.[2] In fact, boys are less likely to graduate from high school and less likely to attend college than girls.[3]

I spoke with a fellow parent at a youth basketball game recently. This dad shook his head, lamenting, "We don't know how to motivate our son to care. He isn't invested in anything. He doesn't work hard to accomplish any long-term goals in sports, or clubs, school—anything. I'm hoping basketball sticks. He's pretty good if he tries, but he is never giving full effort out there." This was an engaged parent. My heart went out to this family because they were genuinely working hard to help their son. Motivation and grit are internal, heart-level qualities that take time to develop. We can't lecture motivation into the hearts of our sons.

How do you develop the tenacity in your son that will serve him the rest of his life? This desire to do so is an important trait for all parents, Christian or not. But for a faithful mama, your desire for him to develop grit comes from a deeper, wider hope. I know your *primary* goal doesn't start and end with mere results. Varsity ball, straight As, Musk-like wealth.

What we're aiming to do as Christian moms is to develop a godly character in our sons. You want his grit on the field, in the classroom, and someday in the workplace to be rooted in genuine faith. We want *godly grit* for our boys. The kind of steadfastness or endurance that isn't only noticeable in school or on the field. This godly grit is

Pervasive, godly grit is rooted in faith, and cultivated through hardship.

rooted in his heart's desire to please God over the long term. You want him to understand and develop endurance that he can apply to every area of his life. Pervasive, godly grit is rooted in faith, and cultivated through hardship.

WHAT THE BIBLE TELLS US ABOUT THIS QUALITY

We rejoice in our sufferings, knowing that suffering produces endurance, and endurance produces character.

Romans 5:3–4 ESV

Here's where we moms need to check our Bible-believing selves against what our culture values. We raise boys in a world that avoids suffering at all costs. Our culture does not rejoice in sufferings—it resents them. Instead, we rejoice in our comfort. This is why a generation of mothers gives in to their sons' spending every minute of free time zoning out on digital entertainment. To the untrained eye, this type of parenting initially appears to have eliminated struggle— ta-da! A cocoon of comfort. Only problem? Nothing worthwhile happens in a cocoon of comfort. To the contrary, a generation of boys raised on tablets and gaming consoles grows into a generation of flat, unmotivated, purposeless young men.

The normal setbacks of life, small and big, are growth catalysts for grit, perseverance, endurance. Help your boys see this perspective by narrating setbacks and growth from a young age. You can do this in the tiniest minutia of the day.

"I see you're trying to build that block tower higher, but can't get past that fifth block without it falling over. Keep trying, buddy. You will get it." Today it's blocks, tomorrow it's riding a bike, next year it's memorizing the catechism. The setbacks develop perseverance. Show him how. Show him examples in his life, yours, or a friend's. Tell him how his favorite athlete became a world-class sports icon: dedication, practice, endurance. Point out the commitment required to achieve a big goal: persevering when training was painful, getting cut from the team, sitting the bench for a whole season, waking up before the sun to lift heavy weights. If you look, you'll see endurance fuels every success worth marveling at. It also fuels our ability to endure the normal ups and downs of everyday life. Whether your son is destined for worldly greatness or not, your work to build his capacity for grit will help his character tremendously.

Think of raising your son as filling his heart and mind through one long conversation, rather than thousands of short ones. I heard this years ago, and it removed the pressure to make every conversation 100 percent meaningful. Sometimes you'll include observations of grit without mention of the gospel explicitly. But look for opportunities to draw from Scripture to show him how endurance is developed, and why it is valuable for both our time on earth and in heaven.

One segue from sports grit to godly grit comes to mind with Paul's words to Timothy, when he tells Christians to "train yourselves for godliness; for while bodily training is of some value, godliness is of value in every way, as it holds promise for the present life and also for the life to come."[4] If your little T-ball or basketball or swimming champ shows growth as a result of hard work, praise that. Then use the opportunity to share the biblical perspective that just as we practice and train for sports to get better, we practice and train in working out our faith to grow stronger spiritually.

> Count it all joy, my brothers, when you meet trials of various kinds, for you know that the testing of your faith produces steadfastness.
>
> James 1:2–3 ESV

If you told your son no, and he was tempted to throw a tantrum but refrained, celebrate it. If he stopped shy of hitting his sister after she poked him, celebrate it. If you see him face a tough situation and respond in obedience—celebrate the heck out of that. A simple verbal praise will do. "Wow, you obeyed me and God when you chose a deep breath over screaming! Great job, buddy! I know that's hard. How does it feel to do the right thing? Every time you practice following God, He is pleased. And you grow!"

A few years ago, I homeschooled our kids for a hot minute. I had grand visions of virtues and rigorous academics I'd impart on my second- and third-graders. Greek and Latin word roots, epic historical narratives, biology. Only problem? My seven-year-old son could not focus for more than six minutes before he was out of his chair: doing headstands, drumming on the table, making weird noises. I wanted to gouge out my eyeballs. Instead, I asked a therapist about it. "He's seven," the therapist said. "Six minutes of seated attention is what he can give right now. Work with what you have. It'll grow."

I didn't particularly like his answer. But I followed the advice, working with the attention span my son had. We accomplished everything God already knew we would. Today, that teenage boy earns straight As, has zero attention problems at school, and excels at French horn and tennis. He grew in endurance as I bore with him patiently in love. (And even sometimes not very patiently. He grew anyway.) The growth takes years, my friend. Take a breath and offer your frustrations up in prayer, for you and your boy.

MOM'S GODLY GRIT IS POWERFUL AND CONTAGIOUS

For you have need of endurance, so that when you have done the will of God you may receive what is promised. . . .

My righteous one shall live by faith,
   and if he shrinks back,
my soul has no pleasure in him.

Hebrews 10:36, 38 ESV

This verse is scary! The last thing I want to be, or want my kids to be, is a person who God's soul "has no pleasure in." God has no pleasure in believers who "shrink back." Shrinking back is the opposite of living by faith. In order to live by faith, we need endurance. Let's live this out and help our boys do it too. As moms constantly addressing the needs of wily little ones who appear to lack survival skills and even common sense, we understand the value of endurance in a tangible way. Moms need endurance to raise godly kids—because it is challenging! We feel guilty sharing the trials of motherhood, but there certainly are plenty. You're not alone. Let's together commit to living by faith through cultivating our own endurance.

> The way is hard that leads to life.
>
> Matthew 7:14 ESV

If you're raising your son by the truth of God's Word, you will encounter hardship. We swim upstream training sons to live godly in a culture that moves further away from the Bible. Not only this, but in our very homes, the day-to-day work required of us to correct and train, to encourage and coach our sons, is HARD. This shouldn't surprise us, because Jesus told us repeatedly that we would face difficulties in this life.[5] But I hope to encourage you as you hope and pray for change in the heart of your son. The right way, the way of Jesus, is difficult! It will be wrought with setbacks and a seeming lack of progress.

As I write, I've been tempted to despair over a child showing zero observable progress in one specific area of character development. I refuse to despair. I will keep moving forward. Because we fix our eyes not on what is seen, but on what is unseen, as we read in 2 Corinthians 4:18, back in chapter 3. We choose faithfulness in the face of hardship. That's what makes a faithful mom; that's what increases our own godly grit. Your son will witness your grit, endurance, and steadfast commitment over the long term. *That* is contagious.

SHARE STORIES TO TEACH ENDURANCE, STEADFASTNESS, GRIT

Random influencers, streamers, and reality stars bombard the cultural conversation about whom to look at and what to emulate.

Don't be a passive spectator to those who influence your son. Feed his heart and mind with examples of grit: godly, secular, athletic, professional. Show him admirable qualities in real people. Acquaint him with character traits you want him to emulate. Here's one biblical example.

Tell your son the story of Noah from Genesis 6:9–8:22. Try the New International Revised Version, as it is very easy for your young boys to understand.

Below is a quick recap, if you want to read it aloud to him.

A long time ago, people were so violent and all they ever wanted was to do evil and to disobey God. Human sin was out of control. God's heart was troubled. He decided to wipe all the sin and evil away. But Noah was faithful and obeyed God. God told Noah He was going to destroy the evil people and earth with a flood. He told Noah to make a giant boat, or an ark, made of cypress wood. He gave Noah very careful directions, telling him exactly how wide and tall it should be. Noah got to work.

Think about this for a minute. The people around Noah didn't trust or obey God. They probably thought Noah was crazy! There he was, building a huge ship on dry land. I'd guess the people laughed at him for working hard to obey a God they ignored. I bet some days Noah was tired. What do you think? How would you feel working on building a big ark while everyone around you made fun of you?

Noah spent years working on the ark, following God's directions. Some people think it took around fifty-five to seventy-five years to build the ark.[6] When the ark was finished, God told Noah and his family to gather lots of animals, males and females of each kind, and plenty of food to load onto the ark.

Finally, the rain came. It didn't stop for forty days and forty nights. Water covered the ground, the trees, and the houses. Noah and his family were safely inside the ark. They had trusted and obeyed God, worked hard, and God protected them. As the rain flooded the earth, I bet those other people wished they'd obeyed God!

Noah finally saw with his eyes what he knew in his heart: Obeying God was worth it. Even when it was hard, and even when the end felt far away. Can you imagine if Noah had given up?

What do you notice about Noah? I notice that he obeyed God, and God empowered Noah to finish his work, even when it was difficult. That's called faithful obedience. I also notice that he was good at completing work that took a long, long time. That's called perseverance, or steadfastness. Some people call that grit. Noah's grit came from a deep faith in God.

FINAL NOTE

If you help him look for it, your son will find endless opportunities to grow in grit. While he might enjoy electronics (they are engineered to addict him), digital entertainment is not a helpful venue for developing the kind of endurance we're after. Hours spent "leveling up" is not helping your son in the long term. Research abounds on the addictive and harmful effects of too much digital entertainment. Help your son learn endurance in the real world, treating digital entertainment like a dessert: okay once in a while, but not as the main course—and not necessary daily. Challenge your son to learn a difficult song on an instrument, make it to the spelling bee, beat his best mile time, build a birdhouse, tackle a tough Lego build, memorize a Scripture passage. Using our gifts to the glory of God here in the real world requires work and perseverance. Praise his effort and determination.

#6 TENDERNESS

The world: "My son enjoys digital entertainment, so that's what he does during his free time. It's fine; that's how all kids play now."

Mission-minded boy mom: "My son needs more real-life experiences with nature, people, and God's Word to help him grow into the kind of person God made him to be. Too much device time blocks these experiences and hardens his heart."

Tenderness is gentleness and kindness that comes from the deep well of the heart. I'm not talking about the obligatory gut-response when you prompt your son to be nice, and he outwardly complies through gritted teeth. (Although teaching and training will certainly result in plenty of that along the way.)

In the next three chapters we are going to peer behind the concept of tenderness, exploring the foundations of a tender heart. What can we instill in our boys that will lead to the development of tenderness? He'll need a great sense of wonder at this big, beautiful world (chapter 16). He'll need to accurately appraise himself in light of God's standard, not the world's (chapter 17). And he must be acquainted with the beautiful concept of grace—undeserved favor (chapter 18). The next three chapters will explore tenderness through these three ideas, and include plenty of tools for growing strong boys who aren't afraid of—but seek after—a soft heart.

WONDER

"WOW!" ISN'T JUST FOR OWEN WILSON

How often we miss the fingerprints of the Artist behind it all because the eyes of our heart are distracted or busy with more temporal demands, the noise of life beckoning us to follow. How different the fruit of a life given to create time for wondering, imagining, reflecting. But it must be sought intentionally; it must be fought for among the constant voices tempting us to the draw of busyness.

—Sally Clarkson, *Awaking Wonder*[1]

The world will never starve for want of wonders; but only for want of wonder.[2]

–G. K. Chesterton, *Tremendous Trifles*

My husband and I went to dinner recently. It was a beautiful night, and a lineup of talented local musicians played on the restaurant's patio, twenty feet away. A father and son sat down at the table next to us. The boy was about eight or nine. From the moment they sat, until the moment they left, this child tapped away on his phone. Not one conversation happened between the boy and his dad. Even when the food arrived, the boy alternated bites with tapping, scrolling, never making eye contact with his dad. The scene broke my heart. All around us, there was beauty to take in: a gentle breeze, blooming and fragrant jasmine plants, a large dog patiently panting beside his owner's table. Not to mention the opportunity to talk with a father who won't be around forever. What is his dad's favorite drink? What jokes make him laugh? What does he do at work? This is a scene the boy doesn't know that he wants etched into his memory. The boy's opportunity to wonder was hijacked by a device. And this same scene is playing out everywhere today.

Your little boy is positively wired for wonder! This is why, from that first glimmer of mobility, he's grabbing at everything, climbing atop Mount Sofa, shoving every small-enough object inside his mouth. Curiosity fuels him. He is 100 percent interested in the world around him. The cat's tail, the ceiling fan, the toilet water. He wants to see, touch, taste, and feel. Everything is new!

For mom, his curiosity can be entirely exhausting.

This is why so many of us tired moms give in to the TV show, the tablet, the video game.

Unfortunately, your son's consumption of digital entertainment is stunting his capacity for wonder.

OUR HURRIED LIFE PACE SQUELCHES WONDER

Our culture values efficiency over depth, outer appearances over inner virtue, and pride over humility. If we don't stop to deliberately choose the opposite, we'll slide right into today's busy status quo, with stacked Jenga-tower schedules. We load up the days with twice-weekly baseball practice, base-running practice,

> We want our sons to have the headspace and calendar space to look around and think about the world that's much bigger than they are.

pitching lessons, and batting instructors. We've stolen our kids' downtime, which is critical for their development, particularly their sense of wonder.

Overloaded calendars create fast-paced days. When downtime does arrive, overscheduled boys don't know what to do with it. They complain of boredom, and we cave, handing them a device. Our boys who are starving for free play are even further removed from the kind of activities that expand their sense of wonder.

We want our sons to have the headspace and calendar space to look around and think about the world that's much bigger than they are. We want them asking questions. *Who made this world? Who made that giant lake? Why does this rock skip when I throw it just right? How high are those mountains in the distance? Where do the geese that fly in Vs wind up?* These questions, spurred by time and reflection, ultimately lead them back to their Creator. Let's look for opportunities to introduce and spur wonder in our sons.

SIMPLE, FUN WAYS TO SPUR YOUR SON TO WONDER

Growing up, my dad and I went on a lot of walks. I remember the sound of the crows flying overhead by the thousands. Dad would crouch down at my eye level, pointing to the birds. "Look," he'd say. "Every night at the same time, they fly into those trees." He drew my attention to whatever there was to notice that day. After the long, steady rains of El Niño, Dad would point out the green hills in the distance, which used to be brown. He called my attention to creation. Sometimes he'd remind me that God made everything we saw. Sometimes he would point out the beauty. He created a practice for me: look, notice, share, remember. You can do the same with your sons as you drive in the car or walk around the block or on a local hiking trail.

Point out the clouds, the change in seasons, the waterways. Listen for animal sounds, birds, bugs. Notice the stars. The vast oceans, smooth meadows, snow-covered hills. Point out the colors, the shapes, the wind. Marvel at the weather changes.

If you're anything like me, maybe you want to show your kids the great, big world, but lugging the family on a safari ain't going to happen anytime soon. If that's the case, use the resources around you to bring the greatness of creation to them.

Planet Earth. Watch this documentary series as a family, and you can tour the remotest places on earth without spending a dime. Note: Sometimes animals are eaten. Use your own judgment on using that fast-forward button. For some kids, such scenes are a great opportunity to explain that this only started when sin entered the world and that when God makes a new heaven and a new earth, animals won't eat each other anymore! For other kids, a simple fast-forward will do.

National Geographic fact books. My sons eat these books up. You can get them in the children's nonfiction section at the library.

Indescribable by Louie Giglio. This is one to add to your library shelf for sure. It's a devotional-style book about creation, ultimately pointing to God as Creator.

"I don't know." This is a powerful phrase for mom to get comfortable using. "Mom, how many gallons of water are in the ocean?" When your son asks a question that you could not possibly know the answer to, tell him so! Wonder alongside him. You're not trying to pretend you know it all; you're showing him that you know the One who does know it all. That's powerful.

Be on the lookout for where your son stops and lingers a little. Near the piano? Watching you cook dinner? Watching dad fix a fence post or brother playing baseball? You'll get beautiful glimpses into his heart from a very young age. Ask him, "What are you thinking about, bud?" See where his mind is headed. Feed his interests to help cultivate his sense of wonder.

Sally Clarkson writes, "Each of us has a capacity to bring light, goodness, beauty, creativity, and love to our world. . . . Believing that we matter and that our lives have meaning" motivates us to use our gifts.[3] Help your son see both the needs of the world and his capacity to bring goodness to it. You'll grow his sense of wonder, purpose, and self-efficacy simultaneously.

PEEK IN TO SEE WHAT HE WONDERS ABOUT

"Hey, guys, I'm curious," I asked my kids on the way to school. "What do you wonder about when you're lying in bed, or when you're outside, looking at the clouds?"

"I wonder what's beyond the universe," Jack, my thirteen-year-old son said.

"That's interesting! Have you read any books that have made you wonder big things, or caused you to stop and think about how big God is?"

"Oh, yes," Jack replied. "The book *Indescribable*. It's incredible. There are so many scientific facts about the world. It's just amazing."

"*Bible Infographics*," my daughter chimed in.

"Definitely agree. Can we get the second one, by the way?" Jack asked.

I was thrilled they liked these fascinating books full of mind-blowing facts and figures in the Bible. "I wonder if I could jump onto the clouds and take a bite," my eight-year-old daughter replied.

"They're just water molecules, you know," said eleven-year-old Carter, popping little sister's dream real quick.

"I know . . . but still," she said, wistfully looking into the sky.

"I wonder about how God is eternal," Carter shared. "It's hard to imagine that time didn't exist before God made it."

"That's definitely a brain-bender, huh!" I replied.

I loved hearing the inner thoughts of my kids. It was so easy to peer inside their hearts, and they were quick to give me a glimpse—when I asked.

Ask your son what he wonders about when it's quiet and calm.

TEACH HIM TO WONDER AT THE CHARACTER, HEART, AND ATTRIBUTES OF GOD

When he's very tiny, he can use his senses to observe God's visible creation. As he grows, he can begin to understand the character attributes of God. The stuff we can't see, necessarily, but we experience daily. As your son grows, share how good, forgiving, kind, gentle, loving, and strong God is. Wonder over His attributes together. Explain that when God says we're made in His image, it doesn't mean that the Father has a face like ours, but it means that we are created to reflect His traits.[4] Everything good in us is both from God and a tiny glimpse of His limitless goodness.

Take everyday moments to behold and wonder at whatever goodness pops into your day, pointing to the ultimate Source of all goodness. Opportunities are there when you look, I promise. Not every conversation needs to connect with a perfect bow, of course. Ask God for opportunities and wisdom for when to share an idea or connection. And whatever you do, don't give up if your attempts aren't received. Just keep going!

If your boy is a toddler, explaining the immutability of God may be over his head. BUT, look for ways to keep it simple! Here are some examples of how you can help introduce this idea of wondering at who God is.

- "I was thinking about how impatient I am sometimes. I remembered that God has been *so* patient with me. I didn't decide to follow Him until I was seventeen years old. For all those years before then, I was disobeying Him. He patiently loved me the whole time. I'm amazed at His patience with me. When I think about His patience toward [insert your example here: Joseph's brothers for selling him to slave traders, the Israelites in the desert who complained nonstop], it's so silly for me to lose all my patience because another driver isn't following the rules. Do you ever struggle to stay patient? Isn't it cool that God's patience is perfect?"

- "Forgiving that boy who hurt you on the playground is so hard. To be honest, I'm having trouble forgiving him too! Especially when he didn't say sorry. Did you know that Jesus forgave us from all our sins—while we were still sinning? *While* He was dying on the cross, He was praying for the people who were crucifying Him! He asked God to forgive them long before they ever thought about being sorry. Isn't that amazing? It's hard for my heart to feel that way toward people who wrong me. No one has ever done anything as wrong to me as that, not even close. I am amazed about how forgiving God is. The more I think about it, the more I want to forgive the people around me."

- "A US Navy SEAL named Michael Monsoor was serving with two other SEALs. The enemy threw a grenade that bounced off Michael's chest and fell to the ground. He yelled, "Grenade!" to alert his friends. Michael was the only SEAL with a clear path to escape. The other two he was with were trapped. Michael could have chosen to run to safety, but instead he jumped on top of the grenade—to absorb the explosion and protect his friends. Michael gave up his life for his friends.[5] This story is true! Jesus said, "No one has greater love than the one who gives their life for their friends."[6] Jesus laid down His own life—for the whole world. Isn't it amazing to think about how much He sacrificed for us?"

There are a zillion ways to make connections aloud between goodness in the world and God. After all, every good and perfect gift is from Him (James 1:17). Living in the real world as devoted followers of Christ means that we will pursue knowing God more. We will fall down and get back up again. Share what you learn about God, as you live out your faith. Fill your son's mind with what God is teaching you in His Word, and in His world. What do you marvel at? What captures your heart?

BIBLE VERSES TO SHARE AS YOUR KIDS OBSERVE THE BEAUTY IN NATURE, AND WONDER ABOUT THEIR CREATOR

There is none like you among the gods, O Lord,
    nor are there any works like yours.
All the nations you have made shall come
    and worship before you, O Lord,
    and shall glorify your name.
For you are great and do wondrous things;
    you alone are God.

Psalm 86:8–10 ESV

Everyone on earth is amazed at the wonderful things you
    have done.
What you do makes people from one end of the earth to
    the other sing for joy.

Psalm 65:8 NIrV

ACCURATE APPRAISAL OF SELF

I'M TALKING ABOUT THE BOY IN THE MIRROR

Her creed was very short. . . . When everything went against her, this was her stay, "My trust is in God. My trust is in God." . . . And if every one had a mother like that mother . . . there would be no use for jails.

—D. L. Moody, speaking at his mother's funeral[1]

Shelby's twin boys were about three years old when she was pregnant—with a second set of twins. (I know. Holy moly, right?) One Saturday morning around Valentine's Day, Shelby and her husband, Dave, attempted to "sleep in." As in, they told the three-year-olds not to get out of bed until 7 a.m., when their special alarm clock lit up green.

Barely after seven, doubly pregnant Shelby walked into her living room to find her sons huddled in the crevice of their L-shaped couch—surrounded by a dozen empty Hershey's Kiss foils.

"What do you think you are doing?" Shelby couldn't believe her eyes.

One of her boys turned his head, face covered in chocolate and still chewing. He looked her dead in the eye and said, "Maybe if you'd made us breakfast . . ."

When Shelby recounted this story, I nearly spat out my coffee laughing. (Our own frustrating parenting stories don't seem funny at the time. But if you add time or change the wild child to somebody else's kid, *then* we can see the humor.) The gumption! The audacity of a small boy to double-down after clearly violating a basic household rule: no chocolate bingeing before breakfast. These boys are nearly grown now. But Shelby and I laughed about how we can see our boys' personalities, the way God wired them, even from toddlerhood.

MOMS HAVE A PERFECT VANTAGE POINT FOR OUR CALLING

We mothers are strategically positioned for one-of-a-kind insight into our children's unique personalities—both their strengths and where they are prone to wander. It is critical to show your son how to accurately assess himself. We've already talked about how to anchor him in his inherent value and unconditional love. But we must also guide him toward a clearer understanding of how he can take responsibility for his mistakes through the hopeful lens of grace. We must help him identify his own sin tendencies, giving him tools to fight against them. And the best part of accurately assessing himself includes helping him enjoy his strengths.

WHERE WE'RE HOPING TO ARRIVE BIG PICTURE: MEASURING OURSELVES AGAINST THE WORD

We want our son to grow into an understanding of his position before God. All have sinned and fallen short of living the perfect life that glorifies God.[2] Sinners will face the consequences of those sins one day. A perfect Judge will weigh each person's life, declaring the fair consequences for every sinful thought, word, and action. This is terrifying.

Thankfully, the perfect Judge is also perfectly loving and doesn't want any of His kids to face hell. That's why He sent His Son to live a perfect life and pay the penalty for all human sin. In the most generous, outrageous gift of all time, God offers eternal life to us—for free—when we place our faith in Christ, confessing with our mouth and believing in our heart that Jesus, God incarnate, came to die for us. When we place our faith in Him, we are justified. Boom—declared righteous before God. Not because of us, but because we've accepted this free gift from Jesus! Our eternity is secure, because when God judges us, he sees Christ's perfect righteousness instead of our sin. The story doesn't end there, because God is sanctifying us—or maturing us—as we serve Him here on earth. We will still sin, but what do we do after we sin? Do we confess it, turn back to God, ask for help overcoming this sin? This is how a believer walks out his faith daily.

Moms are called to preach this gospel to our sons, over and over again. *This* is how they will eventually come to understand the standard by which to appraise themselves, and the grace by which they are able to be saved.

Our hope is that each of our sons begins to see that while he is deeply, unconditionally loved, he is also flawed, prone to sin, and in need of help outside himself.

This concept flies in the face of our cultural narratives in many ways. First, the idea of spiritual, inner neediness is not a popular one. The world tells us we are growing our kids to be fully independent. Yes, we want our son to launch out of the home, hold down a job, and pay his bills, but we never want him to believe the lie that he can live the life God has for him without God.

Second, our world pretends that it's possible for "your truth" and "my truth" to coexist. Unlike subjective observations such as which Thai dish is the best (*phad ka prow*, obviously), objective truth does not change. There is an objectively true standard that we will all be measured by, and it's found in God's Word.

Third, the message of the Bible is inclusive, meaning it is open to everyone who puts their faith in Jesus. But it is also exclusive, in that salvation is only available to those who have embraced the gospel truth of Jesus. The more popular worldly narrative is that "all paths lead to God." This simply isn't true.

We want our sons to understand that the world revolves around God, that we fall short of God's call on our lives, and that through Christ, God wants to do a great work in us. It starts with viewing ourselves from God's truth.

Helping our young boys understand this will take time and intentionality. You can do it!

A BOY WHO COULDN'T SEE HIS SIN WHEN GOD HIMSELF SHOWED HIM

If you grew up going to church, I'm sure you've heard the story of Cain and Abel, Adam and Eve's sons. I reread the account with fresh eyes recently, and something new jumped out at me.

Cain and Abel went into different lines of work. Cain farmed; Abel kept sheep. Cain offered the Lord "the fruit of the ground," while Abel offered God the firstborn of his sheep, and their fat portions. If you know anything about fruit, you know that the fruit that falls to the ground isn't the best fruit—it's the leftovers. The worst. Cain gave God leftovers. Abel, on the other hand, offered to God the most valuable thing he had.

> The LORD had regard for Abel and his offering, but for Cain and his offering, he had no regard.
> Genesis 4:4–5 ESV

Imagine you are Cain, and you gave God a sloppy afterthought of an offering. You look over and see your brother has offered the best, most valuable things he has. I think we'd experience a similar feeling if we showed up at a potluck at the president's house with a bag of rotting fruit, only to look around and see that the other attendees brought gourmet items that had clearly taken much time and effort to prepare. Filet mignon, risotto, chocolate lava cake, lobster tail . . . and then your paper bag of mealy fruit you'd found in the back of your car on your way to the party. My face burns with shame even typing this out! But Cain doesn't burn with shame when he sees the discrepancy in his offering and his brother's. When he realized God was not pleased with his offering, "Cain was very angry, and his face fell" (Genesis 4:5). Cain's heart was hard.

Still, God speaks to him. "Why are you angry, and why has your face fallen? If you do well, will you not be accepted? And if you do not do well, sin is crouching at the door. Its desire is contrary to you, but you must rule over it" (Genesis 4:6–7).

God doesn't reject Cain. He warns him. But Cain doesn't heed God's warning. Instead, Cain murders his own brother out of anger and jealousy. Cain's heart is hard as a rock. He is unteachable, even by God himself!

Two major takeaways as a mom: First, it is possible that despite your best, most faithful efforts, your son's heart will not tenderize. Cain and Abel had the same mom and dad, were raised in the same house, with presumably the same rules and family culture. Yet the boys demonstrated entirely opposite heart postures toward sin, repentance, and obedience to God. So hold on to the truth that the ultimate posture of your son's heart toward God is above your pay grade.

Second, God already knows how this story will end, and He still warns Cain. "Sin is lurking at the door; and its desire is for you, but you must master it." We can't control our sons' heart posture, but we will be held accountable for our faithfulness in training up our sons to love God. We must warn, train, exhort, and teach our boys to follow God. Pray, persevere, and fight to win his heart to the things of God. Especially when he appears to be entirely opposed to the idea.

Let's get practical here and talk about helping your boy grow in tenderness, and into a clear view of himself.

TEACH THE STANDARD

In our culture, we love to compare ourselves to people who *really* blow it. If our standard is murderers and burglars, well, most of us haven't done anything that bad. *So I must be a good person, right?*

One of the most effective ways to show your son his need for grace and forgiveness is to teach him the Ten Commandments. My favorite way to teach this is through song. Download the New City Catechism app on your phone and play the Ten Commandments songs in the car as you drive around. Your three-year-old may not understand every word right now, but you're creating the infrastructure for him to grasp it as he grows. Play it regularly!

You shall have no other gods before me. (God should be the most important thing in your life.)

You shall not make for yourself an idol. (Don't invent an idea of who God is, worshiping that god. Know and worship the one true God.)

You shall not misuse the name of the Lord your God. (Treat God's name with respect and honor.)

Remember the Sabbath day by keeping it holy. (Spend time in rest and worship of God on the Sabbath.)

Honor your father and your mother. (Obeying mom and dad is one of God's laws.)

You shall not murder. (Do not hate, hurt, or kill your neighbor.)

You shall not commit adultery. (God's design for marriage is one man and one woman—for life. If you're married, you can't have a girlfriend too.)

You shall not steal. (Don't take anything that's not yours without permission.)

You shall not give false testimony. (Don't lie.)

You shall not covet. (Be content, not envying anyone else's stuff.)

As you teach these commandments to your son, show him how they personally apply to him. "One way to figure out if you're a 'good person' is to see if you have ever broken God's rules. Have you ever told a lie? Been jealous about a toy someone else had? Hated or hit a friend or sibling? Disobeyed your mom or dad? Loved anything more than God? Oh, no! I've done all these things too! That means we have broken God's laws and will have consequences for our sins. The good news, or gospel, says that Jesus already took those consequences for us. How amazing is that?"

As you help your son see his sin, always point him back to the good news of grace and forgiveness in Christ. This helps make the connection for him in his brain that sin is wrong, yet our confession is met with the grace and forgiveness that Christ offers—should we accept it. Here you have opportunities to shepherd your son the way God shepherds us.

TEACH HIM TO SAY HE WAS WRONG

Nancy, mom to four grown boys and thirteen(!) foster sons, gave me this helpful tip for raising young sons.

Instead of requiring her sons to say, "I'm sorry," she required them to say, "I was wrong to . . ." lie, hit, whatever. Nancy explained it like this: "I can't know if his heart is legitimately sorry for his offense. I hope he will get there. But it was important to me to train my boys to be able to verbalize, 'I was wrong.' Do you know how many grown adults in the corporate world are unable to say those three small words? I wanted to train boys from their youth to be able to admit mistakes."

In a world where we tend to justify our own sin, Nancy gave her boys an important tool that they still use as grown men.

A BOY WHO THINKS TOO LOWLY OF HIMSELF

"I'm not good at anything!" Franz cried to his mom after being cut from the school's basketball team. He slumped to the floor, head in hands.

"Son, that is simply not true," mom Penelope softly replied. "You are great at many things. But much more important than sixth-grade sports is your character. Your willingness to put yourself out there, to try something new? That shows courage. Courage you can take with you everywhere. Basketball season will be over next month."

Franz looked up at his mom through tears. "But why didn't I make the team? Why am I so bad at everything? I'm the worst."

Penelope tried again. "I know this feels really big right now. In the big scheme of your life, you are going to have great days and bad days. Sometimes you win, and sometimes you lose. But the most important things in life never, ever change. God loves you. He made you! And He blew me away when He did! He made you brilliant and hardworking. You are a wonderful friend. Basketball might not be your thing, but you're incredible at swimming! You are funny as heck. God has a reason behind why you didn't make the team. We can trust Him. This is where your faith has a chance to grow. Do we trust Him, even in our hardest days? You get to choose." Penelope pulled Franz closer. She thought Franz was starting to get it, that his heart maybe lifted a little bit?

Franz sat for a moment before exclaiming, "But why didn't I make the team!? Why am I the worst!?" He fell into tears again.

Penelope grew weary.

Sharing this story later with a small group of friends, she said, "I honestly needed a break after an hour of this. I texted my husband to ask how far he was from home because I was about to throw my own pity party." She laughed, and her friends joined her—they could relate.

But through her weariness Penelope clung to the truth: God was doing a work through her, as she spoke life and truth into her son. Franz had a warped view of himself. His feelings eclipsed what was true. And his mom's words were a mirror and an anchor. Even though Franz didn't respond with a lightbulb and a big hug, Penelope's words were shaping, molding, and demonstrating how to coach himself out of a downward cycle by taking his thoughts captive. She knew that throughout this child's life she would be called to speak the same words to him, continuously reminding him of his value as God's child. Each time was good, beautiful, godly work. God was using her, and she prayed that she would one day see the fruit to come.

A BOY WHO THINKS TOO HIGHLY OF HIMSELF

"I am the fastest runner in my whole class, and probably my whole school," kindergartener Clarence boasted to his mom as he climbed into the car and buckled his seat belt.

Mom Margaret knew her son was athletic. Sure, he was fast, but obviously not faster than the kids in the upper grades. She was growing tired of his arrogance. She constantly reminded him of the proverb, "Let another praise you, and not your own mouth,"[3] but the words did not appear to sink into his heart.

Clarence went out of his way to prove he was the fastest, smartest, best at everything. He corrected adults despite being repeatedly chided for it. He always assumed that his way was the best way. Margaret knew that what he really needed was to see himself accurately, and to rearrange his heart's desires. Rather than boasting about himself, Margaret wanted Clarence to lift up others, see his own flaws, value character more than outward performance. She had her work cut out for her.

Margaret looked for opportunities to gently show Clarence that he was not the best at everything.

"How about a timed race?" Margaret suggested one day, when her kids had time to kill in the car while waiting to pick up siblings.

"Yes!" Clarence cried. "I am the fastest."

Margaret timed her kids as they individually sprinted a course she charted. It turned out that Clarence was not, in fact, the fastest of his siblings. She praised their effort and endurance, including Clarence's. Then, without further admonishment, they moved on with their day. Margaret looked for opportunities like this wherever she could find them. She tried as hard as she could to bite her tongue and let these experiences do the talking.

One day, as Margaret made dinner, she peeled garlic by smashing each clove, and pulling off the papers. Clarence, without any cooking or garlic-peeling experience to speak of, told his mom, "That's not how you peel it. I could do it faster."

"Oh?" Margaret bit her tongue for a moment. After more than a decade of preparing meals for her family, if there was one thing she knew, it was how to peel garlic efficiently. "Wash those hands and come on over! Let's race."

Clarence jumped from his seat excitedly, ready to prove his expertise in another realm.

As expected, mom peeled a whole head before Clarence could finish one clove. He smiled at his mom. The boy did have a good nature, taking a loss with understanding. "Well," he shrugged. "Guess it's harder than I thought!"

She smiled at her boy. "Thanks for helping!"

Margaret had several sons. They all had different areas that needed sharpening. She shared her insights with my husband and me after church one day, as we talked about parenting kids who are so differently wired. "It was important that every time Clarence saw that he wasn't the best at everything, I was waiting for him with a reminder that he is cherished and treasured—no matter what place he finishes. I really like to teach lessons to my kids verbally, but I knew that for this child, he would have to see it himself, without my words. Clarence has been a challenge for me, because he is unlike my other boys. While his heart may always tend a little prideful, I have been deeply encouraged by the growth I've seen in him over time,"

Margaret and Penelope faced different challenges with their boys' views of themselves. But one thing they shared in addressing the problems was that each mom valued her son's character and pursuit of godliness more than his external performance, and they both used ordinary things to point back to the bigger picture of God, and growing their sons in Christlikeness.

Another encouragement for us moms, these mothers both conveyed through laughter that their situations were not without stress, frustration, and a seeming lack of progress. Both mothers report continued growth in their sons' characters, and trust that God will multiply their faithfulness. That is a win!

A NOTE ON RECOGNIZING VULNERABILITIES

Accurately appraising ourselves must include a recognition of our vulnerabilities. As you grow in your faith, you certainly become

> We are all serving *something*. We all crave
> affirmation and social validation from *something*.
> Help your son parse out what that something is.

acquainted with your own proclivities to sin. For us moms, we might find that too much time on Instagram brings about feelings of envy, greed, or anxiety. We may find that spending time with our Bible study gals prompts us to pray more, while time spent with the soccer moms tempts us to gossip. It's valuable for us to see where we are vulnerable.

Help your son recognize his own vulnerabilities.

For boys today, a massive vulnerability is time spent online. "Young males are two to three times more likely than females to feel addicted to video games," one study found.[4] The more time our sons invest in gaming and passive digital entertainment, the more susceptible they are to turning inward, exchanging real-world relationships, doing, making, living—for a life of digital dopamine hits. Help your son contextualize this new facet of growing up. When he is small, limit his access to gaming and digital entertainment. As he grows older, explain the hazards: Excessive dopamine released by video games kills our enjoyment of the real world. More time online is less time available to love and serve the people God made for you to love and serve. We are all serving *something*. We all crave affirmation and social validation from *something*. Help your son parse out what that something is. When he's small, this will be more about limiting his access to things that aren't serving his best interests. As he grows, you can have conversations to help him figure this out.

Former president of Facebook Sean Parker admitted concerns about the platform in a 2017 interview, saying, "God only knows what it's doing to our children's brains."[5] He admitted that Facebook and Instagram founders' goal was to create "a social-validation feedback loop . . . exactly the kind of thing that a hacker like myself would come up with because you're exploiting a vulnerability in human psychology."[6]

When we hand over the appraisal of self to culture, our weights and measures wonk out. What does culture value? Is that what you want your son to value in himself? We are fighting an uphill battle. Not every cultural measure is garbage, of course. But we need to pay attention.

Who are your son's heroes? If you don't help him identify this, culture will choose. Provide a stream of positive influences for him to measure himself against. (Note, there are plenty of positive examples even within pop culture! Check out *Hollywood Heroes: How Your Favorite Movies Reveal God* by Frank Turek and Zach Turek.) If you want your son to emulate specific positive examples and not dwell on his vulnerabilities, you'll need to work to limit exposure to the triggers, and amp up the quantity of edifying influences.

ONE LAST ENCOURAGEMENT FOR MOM

When my first child was born, I was determined to make her a genius (lol, I know). Flash cards, reading aloud, counting—I prioritized all of this. You guys, I'm talking about in her first few months of life. I brought her to her six-month checkup and asked the doctor, "Do you think she can count in her head, even if she can't yet verbalize it?"

The doctor looked at me, paused for a moment, and said, "Well, at six months, developmentally babies are just beginning to understand that they are a different entity from their mom."

What? I thought. *All this work, and this baby is only just realizing we're not the same person?!*

I laugh recalling this story for so many reasons. My impatience. My lack of experience and understanding. My priorities as a new mom. But it's a great reminder that growth—spiritual, physical, mental—takes time.

The best moms I know are called to parent some of the most difficult kids. Stay faithful, repeat the truth, and live out your own faith. Accurately appraise yourself, sharing appropriate tidbits with your son along the way—confessing, repenting, joyfully receiving grace.

18

GRACE

GIVING AND RECEIVING

If I have any courage, if I feel prepared to follow my Saviour, not only into the water, but should he call me, even into the fire, I love you as the preacher to my heart of such courage, as my praying, watching Mother.

—Charles Spurgeon[1]

"I hate this entire family!" Ouch. At the end of a long day of parenting through outbursts from this foster child, this felt like a punch in the face. I was out of steam, thanks to the two-hour tantrum leading up to that moment. I was running on empty but had an idea. I suggested we try some deep breathing, which was promptly met with "Shut your stupid face!" Okeydoke.

I tried redirecting, consequences, all the things in my toolbox. But this child's latest comment was the rotten cherry atop a terrible day. I couldn't think of anything else to say. I was weary and defeated. I could only muster, "Well. We love you. We love you when you say mean things, and when you say nice things."

The rest of the kids were quiet for a moment. We all felt the air sucked out of the car. My nine-year-old son chimed in with a hopeful idea: "Look! An opportunity to show Dora grace!"

Cue my tears. Over the past few weeks, we had been singing the song "Amazing Grace" on the way to school. I took each line and explained it. I told them that *grace* meant unmerited favor. I explained that *unmerited* meant undeserved. I urged them to look for opportunities to show grace to the people around them. At the time, these lessons seemed to fall on deaf ears: books thrown, one kid scratching another, someone dropping their toast to the floor, tears ensuing. *Why do I even try?* I remember thinking, exasperated.

Days later, the truth I knew in my heart revealed itself, when I was at the end of my rope. The seeds we plant MATTER. Teaching kids to give and receive grace was important, and it was working. No, they won't nail it every time. But teaching our need for grace—and reminding them to dole it out—is critical and life-changing for our kids. Best of all, here in the real world, opportunities abound to show grace to people who don't deserve it.

LOOK FOR STORIES OF GRACE GIVEN AND RECEIVED TO SHARE WITH YOUR SON

We all know the familiar hymn "Amazing Grace." Did you know the story behind the man who wrote it, John Newton? Newton grew up as a rebellious, foul-mouthed boy who rejected the faith his mother tried to impart before her death when he was almost seven. He continued on this delinquent path, even attempting to talk Christians out of the faith they held. He grew up and worked on ships, eventually profiting off the slave trade, until God changed his heart. Newton's conviction and grief over his sin was met with the grace of God, which moved him to become a faithful follower of Jesus and a minister. He lamented over the harm he had inflicted through the slave trade, and eventually worked to help abolish it.

The limitless, unstoppable grace of God set Newton free from the sin that condemned him. And he wrote the classic hymn:

> Amazing grace! how sweet the sound,
>   That saved a wretch; like me!
> I once was lost, but now am found,
>   Was blind, but now I see.[2]

God's grace sets us free from our sins. Newton tasted this grace, the only freedom available from the weight of his sins: participating in the atrocities of slavery, dissuading believers from faith, years of living in rebellion. As soon as he understood his guilt, his need for saving, Newton understood the sweetness of grace offered to him by God.

Grace is undeserved favor.

> For by grace you have been saved through faith. And this is not your own doing; it is the gift of God, not a result of works, so that no one may boast.
>
> Ephesians 2:8–9 ESV

> Where sin increased, grace increased all the more.
>
> Romans 5:20

And as sinners, our only hope is God's grace. When we receive grace that we did not deserve, we can operate from a place of humility. We understand what God has done for us, and how He calls us to extend grace to the people around us.

Look for examples of grace in your life—when someone forgave you, when you forgave someone else. Share these with your son.

Look for opportunities to celebrate when your son shows undeserved kindness to another person.

Look for opportunities to celebrate when he shows undeserved kindness to another person. Explain how that reflects God's character. Explain how God's way is different from our culture's tendency to cancel and shame people who make a mistake or sin. God offers grace and forgiveness to people instead. He calls us to live that way too. God's way is always better!

BIBLE VERSES TO READ TOGETHER ABOUT GRACE

As each has received a gift, use it to serve one another, as good stewards of God's varied grace.

1 Peter 4:10 ESV

So, chosen by God for this new life of love, dress in the wardrobe God picked out for you: compassion, kindness, humility, quiet strength, discipline. Be even-tempered, content with second place, quick to forgive an offense. Forgive as quickly and completely as the Master forgave you. And regardless of what else you put on, wear love. It's your basic, all-purpose garment. Never be without it.

Colossians 3:12 MESSAGE

ENCOURAGEMENT FOR MOM

Moms working to help their kids understand and practice grace will experience lots of face-palming on a daily basis. If your house is anything like ours, you'll watch scenes play out among your children that resemble *The Office*, childhood edition. Your son takes his brother's hat unapologetically, then complains about his brother using his special pencil. He can't see the irony. Welcome to the club. Every time you call him to extend grace, every time you remind him to notice where he has been shown grace, and every time you extend grace to him, you are faithfully depositing truth into his soul. The growth may be invisible to your eyes right now, but your faithfulness is always seen by God. Keep going!

#7 CREATIVITY

The world: "I need to keep my son busy. If he's bored, he'll get into trouble. That's why I schedule activities for all his free time."

Mission-minded boy mom: "Boredom and time spent outside are nutrients for my son's creativity. This time spurs him on to free play, which results in mental, emotional, and physical benefits."

Human beings are wired to create. Unleash your son's creativity simply through time spent outside. Let him experience the gift of boredom. In the next two chapters, I will share practical ideas for growing your son's creativity. Do not stress if today he would rather be passively entertained than create something. Read the following pages to find out how to get from status quo to mini Van Gogh.

19

GET OUTSIDE

THE BEST PLACE FOR OUR CUTEST WRECKING BALLS

> When playtime was shortened, pulled indoors, and over-supervised, boys lost more than girls.
>
> —Jonathan Haidt, *The Anxious Generation*

When I was in college, right around when the internet was invented but before social media, we used to share funny stuff via email. One day someone forwarded me a viral joke email. It read something like this:

Purchase a Bonsai Kitten today!

Do you enjoy the cuteness of kittens, but don't want to deal with the litter box mess and upkeep? Get a Bonsai Kitten! (Photo of a tiny, precious kitten confined in a jar too small for it.)

Kittens are placed in these glass containers while still tiny. Their bodies grow into the shape of the container, and they can be displayed without any upkeep! They stay in the jar forever!

Obviously, this was a joke. I remember the outrage of a coworker before she realized that it was fake. "This is not right! They're designed to be active, to play. They need to move and stretch and explore! This is torturing our little furry friends!" I explained that it was a joke, and we had a good laugh.

But think about this for a moment: Kids today spend less time outside *per week* than kids one generation ago spent outdoors *per day*. I'm talking only four to seven minutes per day spent on unstructured outdoor play.[1] Kids today spend most of their free time sitting still, looking at a device. Eight- to twelve-year-old boys spend five and a half hours per day on a device.[2] You guys. We're raising a generation of bonsai children. But instead of furry bodies adapting to a jar, our boys' brains are adapting to passive consumption. They're uncultivated, lacking resilience because they haven't spent childhood flexing those muscles. Like my coworker said all those years ago, it's not right. These little guys are designed to be active, to play. They need to move, stretch, and explore. The status quo is detrimental to their health.

A professor of kinesiology refers to this trend as "containerized kids."[3] Rather than running, climbing, and playing outside, kids are confined to car seats, high chairs, and strollers more often and for longer periods of time than previous generations of kids.[4] Parents' intentions may be good—they don't want their kids to get hurt. But in the name of safety, kids are being deprived of the important kind of outdoor, risk-taking play that they need to grow.

In addition to the physical cost of not enough time outside, our boys' mental health can suffer when they spend too much time indoors. The same generation that said goodbye to time outside said hello to forty hours per week of passive digital entertainment. We

Getting your son outside can improve his health and mood, and increase his sense of wonder. Best of all, it's simple and free.

know too much time spent on these devices harms mental health. Studies show that spending time in and around nature is beneficial to children's stress levels.[5]

Here is the good news: Getting your son outside can improve his health and mood, and increase his sense of wonder. Best of all, it's simple and free.

A NATURE-CHILD REUNION

Richard Louv, founder of the Children & Nature Network, says that children today are suffering from nature-deficit disorder, and he calls for a reunion between kids and nature.[6] We've talked about the cost to our sons' physical and mental health when they do not get enough time outside.

I'm going to share ideas for what to *do* outside. But before that, you have to know what incredible changes and learning happen in your son's heart and brain when you simply open the back door or walk to a park or empty field. Check out some of these facts about time spent outside:

- Planning, negotiating, multitasking, and problem-solving are honed when kids play outside in unstructured play. (Meaning without mom planning the game or intervening unnecessarily.)
- Playing outside builds confidence. We learn what we are capable of by taking risks. As much as we want to keep them safe, our boys need to take risks, even when they're little. Scrapes will happen. He will survive. Show your little daredevil that he can brush it off and try again. This skill will serve him the rest of his life.
- Outside time improves vision. One study showed that children who play outside regularly have better distance vision than kids who spend more time inside. (Playing outside develops all the senses, whereas gaming or

passively watching videos only requires two senses: hearing and sight.)[7]

- Time outside prevents and treats ADHD symptoms. Kids with ADHD who spend significant time outside show fewer symptoms.[8]

- Outside time helps restore sanity for mom. Analysis of more than one hundred studies showed that the average boy is more active than 69 percent of girls.[9] Spare yourself another broken lamp, my friend. Take your little wrecking ball outside.

- Our bodies need sun (not too much, but we do need some) to make vitamin D. Vitamin D is needed for bone development and to help our immune system, for sleep and mood.[10]

- Did you know that almost one-third of children in the United States are either overweight or obese?[11] Over the past four decades, childhood obesity has tripled.[12] More boys are obese than girls, and obesity in boys is increasing faster than obesity in girls.[13]

These are all great reasons to crank up the time our boys spend outside. To take it a level deeper, as Christian moms, the most fundamental desire of our hearts is for our kids to know and follow Jesus. Taking your son outside opens the door to great conversations about creation, and God as Creator.

Time outside teaches our little dudes about the nature of God, even before mom explains the connection of creation to Creator. Outside, your son uses his sight, hearing, touch, smell, taste (wisely, mom hopes). He wonders why the tree that lacked leaves last month is now bursting with flowers. He notices the sun rise each morning, only to set again in the same spot as yesterday. He hears the birds chirping in the day but wonders why the sounds change at night.

You want your son to ask these questions, and you definitely want him asking you. God gave you the job of mothering, aka teaching him. Answer those questions the best you can, pointing out the marvelous and magnificent ways that creation blows your mind.

My sister pocket-dialed me fifteen or so years ago. She was driving her three-year-old daughter and infant son around. I said "Hello" a few times before realizing the call was accidental. I listened for a moment to the quiet, when I heard her say, "Guys, look at those clouds. Aren't they so beautiful? . . . God made those clouds." That glimpse into her intentionally pointing her toddler to a Creator—it reminded me of our dad.

Mom Caitlin shared that her own mother would point out gorgeous sunsets to her when she was a child. Caitlin's mom used to say, "Thank God for eyes to see this incredible view." What a lovely prompt to glorify God as we take in nature's beauty.

We can teach this to our boys, passing along the appreciation of the beauty around him, and pointing him to look behind it—to the Maker of the sun, the sea, the line of ants in the lawn.

SIMPLE OUTDOOR PLAY TIPS

Structure in daily yard exploration time. Before lunch, after lunch, after nap, whatever. If he initially protests, keep trying. Don't be surprised if this quickly becomes your son's favorite time of day.

Instead of asking, "Do you want to play outside?" declare, "It's time to play outside!" If he whines, stay strong. Go with him. Get him started. "Look, here are the bubbles/sand toys/water buckets." Plan to stay for a specific chunk of time, regardless of whining. "We're going to spend ten minutes/a half hour/whatever out here, so you can either make it fun, or you can make yourself sad."

Change how you hear "I'm bored." Your child's boredom is not a problem for you to fix. Rather, it's an indicator light showing you that he's hit a wall and needs to use his brain to come up with an idea. This is a great opportunity for him to plan, think, explore.

Pet care. Playing with or walking Fido is a great way to enjoy the outdoors and love on your family pet.

Become a tourist in your own town. Look up local hikes or outdoor attractions and walk or bike there. Take note of what you see, and ask your son what he sees.

Look into a membership at your local zoo. This was one of my favorite outings when I had a gaggle of young kids at home. My friends and I would pack lunches and meet there, and before we knew it the whole morning had gone by. Our kids enjoyed dozens of animals—and by noon they were ready for a nap.

Get a tracker from 1000 Hours Outside. Your kids can track their hours on a coloring page. Set a goal for the year, to spend a thousand hours playing outdoors. The wonderful Ginny Yurich has created great resources for families. Check out her website or Instagram.

YOU MIGHT FIND A LIZARD IN THE LAUNDRY

It was 9:30 p.m. I just wanted to go to sleep, but my son's gym clothes needed to dry before school the next morning. I moved the clothes to the dryer, like one of those good-housekeeper moms who doesn't allow mildew to grow on clean laundry. (Admittedly out of character for me.)

And there he was, tucked into a big shirt: a lizard. Well, more accurately, it was half a lizard. The top half. Needless to say, after washing, rinsing, and spinning—he was not alive.

If it had been my first rodeo, I'd probably have screamed. But it wasn't. So I simultaneously removed and disposed of our reptilian friend (RIP), cleaned up the crime scene, and announced across the house, "Did everyone brush their teeth?"

My kids play outside *a lot.* One thing I can tell you for sure is that more time spent outside will inevitably mean more holes in jeans, more grass stains, more rocks in pockets, and sometimes, a random unwanted pet. Still, I promise you, the mess is worth it.

BIBLE VERSES ABOUT NATURE AND OUTDOORS

Memorize or read these aloud to your son to remind him where the natural wonder and beauty comes from.

Through him all things were made; without him nothing was made that has been made.

John 1:3

In his hand is the life of every creature
and the breath of all mankind.

Job 12:10

He owns the deepest parts of the earth.
The mountain peaks belong to him.
The ocean is his because he made it.
He formed the dry land with his hands.

Come, let us bow down and worship him.
Let us fall on our knees in front of the LORD our Maker.
He is our God.
We are the sheep belonging to his flock.
We are the people he takes good care of.

Psalm 95:4–7 NIrV

BOREDOM

"IF YOU'RE REALLY THAT BORED, YOU CAN FOLD THIS BASKET OF LAUNDRY"

In the beginning, God created . . .

—Genesis 1:1 NASB

Kids today have more toy/game/activity options than any generation before. At the same time, boredom complaints have skyrocketed. One clinical psychologist and boredom researcher points to the rapid rise of digital entertainment as the cause behind the boredom epidemic. "Humans have become used to doing less to get more, achieving intense stimulation at the click of a mouse or touch of a screen."[1]

Our digital entertainment systems have hijacked our kids' dopamine response systems. Electronics entertainment is engineered to release excessive amounts of dopamine (the feel-good neurotransmitter) in the brain. There is so much dopamine released by games and apps that dopamine receptors are dying. This means that kids will require bigger hits of dopamine to experience the same level of enjoyment they once had from less dopamine. The problem with this is that the dopamine released by real-life activities—fishing, playing catch, cards—cannot compete with the excessive amounts of dopamine released through the devices. This is why your kids complain of boredom if they are accustomed to online playtime. This is why it is so difficult to sustain their attention on non-screen activities. And probably why you cave, giving him another thirty minutes—so that you don't have to listen to the boredom complaints.

Here is what you need to remember from the last chapter, because it is true, albeit countercultural: Your child's boredom is not a problem for you to solve. It is an opportunity for your son to practice his boredom negotiation skills. Through this practice, your son will develop problem-solving skills and he'll better hone interests beyond the devices. His creativity will explode. Boredom is an opportunity.

Maybe that sounds nice as you read it on the pages of this book, but when reality hits, you feel differently. If you prompt your son to try a new activity, and he whines, and you're annoyed—you'll need to decide to cling to what is true about the cultural status quo. The plain truth is that going along with the cultural trend—handing your son a device so you don't have to deal with his boredom complaints—may be easier in the moment. But you must reject this style of parenting.

Using digital entertainment to avoid boredom is like putting your overweight dog in a stroller whenever he gets tired on a walk.

Kids who troubleshoot their boredom are kids who are developing their gifts, and learning the way God wired them.

I know from experience. After parenting my own kids according to the cultural digital norm, I finally took away all their devices. Lo

> **Kids who troubleshoot their boredom are kids who are developing their gifts, and learning the way God wired them.**

and behold, instead of citing a video game as a favorite hobby, we now have avid readers, pianists, a French horn player, a budding writer, an animal whisperer, and a remarkable artist. These kids rarely complain of boredom since learning how to respond to it. This story is not unique to my family and has proven universally true for all families who have taken a break from their devices and let their kids wrestle with their own boredom. (For more on how to do this, you can read *Digital Detox: The Two-Week Tech Reset for Kids*.)

WHY ANOTHER SPORT ISN'T ALWAYS THE ANSWER TO BOREDOM

Your child has a .0296 percent chance of becoming a professional athlete.[2] Your child has a 100 percent chance of standing before Jesus.

I don't know about where you're raising your family, but where I live, youth sports are a big deal. Like, if you don't join a baseball travel team by age ten, you likely won't have a shot at the high school team. Loading up our kids' schedules with travel ball, hitting lessons, pitching lessons, and base-running lessons might seem to kill two birds with one stone: boost his chances to excel at his sport, and minimize his downtime. Win-win, right? But can I encourage you to use wisdom and caution as you commit activities to your family's schedule?

Team sports can be deeply beneficial to your son's development. Teamwork, training, grit, endurance, friendship—all good things. But there are two considerations we should bear in mind before we load up the schedule.

First, did you know that seven in ten kids drop out of youth sports by age thirteen?[3] According to the American Academy of Pediatrics, kids are burning out due to overscheduling and excessive training, plus the loss of free play time.[4] Even if you were hoping to give your child an advantage in the sports world, overscheduling him may be counterproductive.

Second, and more important, we can gauge family priorities by how we spend our time, talent, and treasure. Looking at the bank account and calendar tells you all you need to know about a family's priorities. Based on how you spend those assets, what are you teaching your son is most foundational to your family? Sure, it's possible to play on travel teams and take extra lessons to the glory of God. But we are wise to assess our commitments through a biblical lens.

PROVIDE ABUNDANT MATERIALS

Allowing your son to negotiate his boredom teaches planning, executive functioning, social skills—and is less work for mom in the long run. Put him in situations where you are deliberately not orchestrating his activity but you *are* giving him materials to use his creativity, as you complete your own chores or work nearby. Here are a few ideas for simple materials you can provide your son to help his creativity flourish.

Kinetic sand

Uncooked rice in a bin with measuring cups/spoons

Cookie sheet with salt for making shapes/letters/pictures

Paper and pencil or crayons

Paper towel rolls, colored construction paper, tape, glue sticks, scissors

Empty boxes, coloring supplies, tape

A blank notebook and a pencil

Leaves, sticks, rocks

Play dough

A tree

A sandbox

Dirt and a shovel

An empty wrapping paper tube and coloring supplies

Instruments

A bowl of water and a paintbrush (to use outside on concrete)

A note card, an envelope, and a pencil

If your son tends to declare all activities boring, try the classic two-choices method. It goes like this: "I hear you saying you're bored. You could either clean your room or you could have this empty Amazon box and some markers to see what you could make with it." Now he feels like he is getting the better end of the deal when he chooses to make something. And he's learning that he enjoys making a spaceship or car or mailbox.

Your young son can't possibly know his interests without some boredom in the real world. Your job is to create the space for that. "Interests are *not* discovered through introspection. Instead, interests are triggered by interactions with the outside world. The process of interest discovery can be messy, serendipitous, and inefficient. This is because you can't really predict with certainty what will capture your attention and what won't. . . . Without experimenting, you can't figure out which interests will stick, and which won't."[5]

Uncovering our son's wiring requires that he interact with the world. Mom facilitates this by giving him plenty of basic materials—things you already have in your house and yard—and the time and space to interact with them.

Expect messy, expect serendipitous, expect inefficient. And expect his creativity to explode.

BOREDOM → CREATIVITY → MOTHERLY INSIGHT

As your son practices negotiating his boredom, watch what he gravitates toward in his downtime. Where does he linger a little longer? Building? Cooking? Drawing? Writing? Sports? Music? Notice his interests and talents. Use that insight to fuel his creativity even more. Maybe your little guy shoots hoops like Steph Curry himself. Maybe he wants to tinker on the piano more than your other kids. Use that insight to decide how to invest in his talents. As we root in truth and prayerfully observe our boys, I believe the Holy Spirit will guide our insight and decisions.

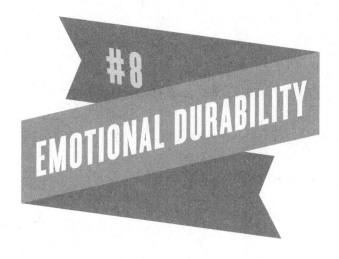

#8

EMOTIONAL DURABILITY

The world: "Boys shouldn't cry or express emotions. My son needs to check his feelings at the door."

Or, on the other end of the spectrum . . .

"He didn't feel like finishing practice, so I picked him up early. I just want my son to be happy."

Mission-minded boy mom: "My son needs to understand his feelings to know when and how they can inform his decisions. I will teach him how."

We can teach our sons to understand and voice their emotions. We can also teach them how to process emotions in a healthy way. Since we're raising boys in a world where rates of childhood anxiety and depression are higher than ever, we must help our sons develop resilience in this area. Emotions can be a gift on a good day, and they don't need to debilitate us on a bad one. In the last three chapters, we will cover how to give your son language for those feelings (chapter 21), help him grow in gratitude as he uses his mind to speak truth into feelings (chapter 22), and give him the gift of rest (chapter 23).

LANGUAGE FOR FEELINGS

BEYOND SHOUTING, STUFFING, AND BLAMING

During the days of Jesus's life on earth, he offered up prayers and
petitions with fervent cries and tears.

—Hebrews 5:7

Sheila's foster son Frank endured severe early childhood loss and
trauma, all before his third birthday. From the day he entered her
home at three years old, he retold his tragic story daily, to anyone
willing to hear it: to Sheila, to her husband, to teachers, to the cashier
at the car wash. The way it appeared, Frank used his severe trauma
as a casual conversation starter. He would recount the specific circumstances, and he would do so matter-of-factly. Sheila scratched
her head about how best to handle this. On the one hand, she wanted
Frank to be able to talk about anything, whenever he needed to. On
the other hand, indiscriminately retelling a harrowing true story of

loss seemed a poor way to process pain. (Not to mention socially awkward.)

Sheila told her foster son's therapist about the situation. The therapist was not surprised, because Frank had shared his story with her many times. During their next session, the therapist waited until Frank brought up his story. After he did, she nodded and said, "That sounds really hard. How does that story make you *feel* when you tell it?"

Frank played in silence for a minute before responding, "It makes me sad."

"I can understand why it would make you sad. That's a hard thing you went through. How else do you feel about it?" the therapist asked.

He grew quiet again. After a few more minutes he responded, "I don't want to talk about this anymore."

The therapist explained to Sheila, "He's trying to process his grief, but he doesn't know how. When he recounts it, let him. Then ask how it made him feel. Then listen. When he can verbally connect the events to his feelings, he can begin to heal."

After years of this practice, the little boy stopped recounting his story with strangers and passersby. When he did bring it up with Sheila and her husband, he began to show and share his emotions along with the events. He began to heal.

According to Dr. Dan Siegel, naming our emotions functionally calms us down.[1] There is complex neuroscience to support this. Dr. Siegel refers to this idea as simply "Name it to tame it."[2] When I heard Dr. Siegel teaching this concept, I thought about Sheila's story of her foster son Frank. I also thought about the 150 psalms in the Bible, written thousands of years ago, that are essentially feelings road maps: The psalmist names his circumstances and emotions, brings them before God, and prays himself back into worship.

Most of the psalms follow a similar pattern: First, a pouring out of raw emotion (often surprisingly raw) to God. Next, the psalmist reminds himself what is true about God. Then, he brings himself

> We want our sons to experience the freedom to recognize and name their emotions, understanding them as indicators, as we teach our boys how to proceed in light of them.

back to the truth of who God is, ending with faith and worship. The book of Psalms provides a path to experience the range of anxiety, grief, lament, joy—in a God-honoring way. Every time I read through Psalms, I am struck by the honesty of the psalter, asking myself, "Can we actually say this to God?" Yes! In His very Word He shows us the scope of human feeling *and* provides a way to process them rightly. He is bigger than our emotions, so we can bring them to Him!

Our culture mistakenly goes two ways with feelings for males. Either we expect them to hide their emotions, or we allow emotions to pilot the ship. As moms, we want our sons to experience the freedom to recognize and name their emotions, understanding them as indicators, as we teach our boys how to proceed in light of them.

ROOT HIM IN BIBLICAL TRUTH, AND GIVE HIM A PLACE TO PROCESS VULNERABLY

As we learned in the introduction, two-thirds of young men ages eighteen to twenty-three say "No one really knows me."[3] We might be tempted to write that off as boys being generally less social than girls. But consider this: Since 1990, the share of young men who lack a single close friend has increased *fivefold*.[4] The *Los Angeles Times* article citing this study acknowledged that digital entertainment is facilitating boys' withdrawal, but there's something bigger behind this epidemic: "They're seeking purpose in a changing world, one in which women are outpacing them in school and work."[5] How can a mission-minded mom help buffer her son from this trend of young male loneliness? Well, for one thing, she can take confidence in the fact that raising boys with a biblical understanding of manhood is in itself a buffer. "Boys with progressive views of manhood feel the least purpose in life."[6]

God designed male and female with unique differences, which are to be celebrated. Men have different muscle mass, are generally stronger, larger, and more physically able to dominate. There are biological differences between men and women. Used as intended, this is how SEAL teams perform strenuous and impressive acts of valor, and is why, when I hear a noise in the middle of the night, I am glad that my husband is the one who gets up to investigate. Human sin can mar the original design, of course. What God has made for our good, some men have used to abuse and harm. We are right to call that out. But let's be precise in what we should be condemning. It's not *maleness*. It's the human twisting and poisoning of God's good design for maleness. How grateful I am for God's design that men love God, and use their strength to protect and defend their families.[7] I flourished as a child under a loving male provider and protector, and I enjoy the same benefits of a godly husband today. A society that denies male/female differences exist, or that demonizes those differences, will be a society in which men suffer from purposelessness.

One caricature of maleness is the false idea that boys and men shouldn't share their vulnerabilities and feelings. I'm not sure where this concept came from. But the research shows that males who have tested the waters by sharing vulnerably and been shut down for sharing have then walled themselves off from the world. What a terrible thing. Vulnerable sharing is the bedrock of both human relationships and a robust faith!

No wonder swaths of young men are suffering from feelings of purposelessness, when our culture denies their natural bent that is beneficial and good for society. (When it is cultivated and anchored in truth.) Men who believe their masculinity is toxic are trapped in self-loathing. No wonder they're wanting to numb out on digital entertainment and pornography.

We want more for our boys.

You are the first and most frequent person with whom your son will risk sharing his vulnerabilities. Give him a place to do this, while providing context for when and where he might need to wait to process in an appropriate way. Give him language for his feelings so he can name and tame them.

HOW TO PRACTICALLY HELP YOUR SON PROCESS EMOTIONS

"One day my young son shouted, 'Ugh! I hate feelings!'" Nancy told me.

"I knew we needed to address this. Feelings aren't all bad! I made it a priority to teach my sons to identify stress, to name it, and how to deal with it in a healthy way. If he can't process emotions, he will turn to secret sin," she told me.

I appreciated her powerful observation and commitment to give her boys the tools they needed to navigate all the feelings. This is our goal. How does it look in the real world, with tiny little boys who are still employing tools like calling their sibling a "doody head"? Time, repetition, and conversation! Let's get specific.

Narrate your own feelings. Lord knows that throughout an average day, we all ride a roller coaster of emotions. A therapist told me that narrating our own emotions is a great way for kids to learn to name their feelings, and walk themselves back into truth despite their feelings. "I am *so* frustrated at that car in the front of the drop-off line. She thinks the line is a personal parking space, so all these families waiting to drop their kids off are going to be late! I'm having trouble loving this neighbor right now. Man, she's making me mad. . . . Lord, will you help my heart to love people who are acting selfishly? And will you show me places where sometimes I act selfishly too? Thank you for forgiving me for my own selfishness. Help me to extend that forgiveness to this driver. Amen."

Use story to identify characters' feelings. You can do this with Marvel movies, bedtime stories, Bible stories—literally any situation retold is an opportunity to ask, "How do you think Adam felt after he disobeyed God and ate the fruit that God said not to eat? Maybe embarrassed? Or ashamed? That would explain why he tried to hide himself."

Use sibling or friend conflict. During conflict, ask your son to identify the other person's feelings based on his or her facial expression and/or words. "Look at Billy's face. How do you think he feels after you hit him? What do you think you could do to make it right?"

A HELPFUL VISUAL FOR MOM AND SON ALIKE

In their book *The Coddling of the American Mind*, Greg Lukianoff and Jonathan Haidt share a helpful picture for navigating the emotions in our minds. They use the metaphor that the mind's processes are like an elephant with a rider.

> The rider represents . . . language-based thinking . . . that we can control to some degree. The elephant represents everything else that goes on in our minds, the vast majority of which is outside of our conscious awareness. . . . [T]he rider often believes he is in control, yet the elephant is vastly stronger, and tends to win any conflict that arises between the two. . . . [T]he rider generally functions more like the elephant's servant than its master, in that the rider is extremely skilled at producing post-hoc justifications for whatever the elephant does or believes.[8]

Our aim is to help our sons learn to train their elephants. If we can identify and name the underlying emotion or reasoning, we can speak to the elephant, ask questions, and examine whether his responses and conclusions are based on fact or fiction. "Over time, the rider becomes a more skillful trainer, and the elephant becomes better trained."[9]

This, Haidt and Lukianoff write, is the concept underlying cognitive behavioral therapy.

This might even remind you of Paul's admonition to "take captive every thought to make it obedient to Christ."[10]

When we examine our thoughts and feelings instead of allowing them to drive the ship, we empower ourselves to be driven by truth, not by the world's mantra of "follow your heart," which is an absolute snare. The Bible tells us the heart is "more deceitful than all else and is desperately sick."[11]

Another helpful tool offered by Lukianoff and Haidt is a list of common cognitive distortions.[12] This may be useful for your own emotional sorting *and* for naming and taming when your kids' or friends' emotions are leading them astray. Below I highlight a few of the terms and explanations on Lukianoff and Haidt's list of distortions, along with my own parenthetical examples of what our boys might be thinking or saying in each case.[13]

RECOGNIZING COMMON COGNITIVE DISTORTIONS

You are **mind reading** when "you assume that you know what people think without having sufficient evidence of their thoughts."[14] (*He thinks I'm a slow runner, that's why he doesn't want to play with me.*)

Catastrophizing finds you believing "that what has happened or will happen will be so awful and unbearable that you won't be able to stand it."[15] (*I can't have ice cream for dinner? This is the worst day of my whole life. Guess I'll move to Australia.*)

Most of us recognize **blaming:** "You focus on the other person as the source of your negative feelings, and you refuse to take responsibility for changing yourself."[16] (*It's your fault I'm sad; you won't let me eat gum from under the seats at school.*)

And what about **what if?** That's when you "keep asking a series of questions about 'what if' something happens, and you fail to be satisfied with any of the answers."[17] (*What if no one wants to play with me?*) My favorite antidote to this is to bring your son back to the gospel truth by encouraging him to swap out "what if" with "even if." Then add a truth that you've instilled in your son about his value and purpose. (***Even if** no one wants to play with me, I know I'm fully known and loved by God and by my family.*)

A LOFTY GOAL FOR LITTLE DUDES

Teaching our boys how to process and understand their emotions must include giving them tools to speak truth and wisdom into their own mind and heart. Taking our feelings to the Lord may affirm our feelings, *or* it may show us that our feelings are distorted.

> I am . . . **the truth**.
>
> John 14:6,
> emphasis added

> I, the LORD, search the heart,
> I test the mind.
>
> Jeremiah 17:10 NASB

> Whatever is true, whatever is honorable, whatever is right, whatever is pure, whatever is lovely, whatever is of good repute, if there is any excellence and if anything worthy of praise, dwell on these things.
>
> Philippians 4:8 NASB

Truth is a lifeline for all of us when our emotions threaten to lead us astray. As believing moms, we know that truth is found in God's Word. We can help our boys identify and then parse out their feelings by listening, and by speaking truth to them. Not because our feelings are always wrong. They can be useful indicators. But we must check them against truth to know. We look to Jesus to see what He did with His own feelings. He brought them to the Father. We can too.

WHAT TEACHING BOYS LANGUAGE FOR EMOTION LOOKS LIKE IN THE REAL WORLD

"This is the worst day of my life!" my five-year-old exclaimed, on our way home from the zoo, Jamba Juice in hand.

"Well, if a fun day with animals plus your favorite smoothie is the worst day of your life, you must have a pretty good life," I replied, mostly for myself.

Why was he upset? Because I declined his request for a playdate with his buddy. It was getting late, bro was tired, and I was tired. We'd already packed the day to the brim. The playdate would need to wait.

"It's your fault I'm sad," he cried, salting his Jamba with his tears.

These moments always try my patience. I took a breath to maintain composure and to make sure I didn't say something I'd regret. He needed me to speak a little truth into his raging elephant brain.

"Here's what I've noticed about today. In the morning, I packed your lunch, then packed up the car, and drove to the zoo. I watched you laugh and smile and play for hours. I loved our time together. Then you got a special treat that you enjoy but don't get to have often. And at the end of this day, you're saying it wasn't just a bad day, but the *worst* day? Could it be that it *was* a great day, but that you want more?"

He sat quietly.

"From my perspective, it was a good day, but you are lacking gratitude. When I see my kids don't have gratitude, that shows me they don't need *more*; they need *less*."

"No!" he yelled.

I could tell more words wouldn't help us at this point. So I turned up the radio, and we drove home. Over the course of the next couple of years, that same child would use the same simple declaration when the day didn't go his way. "Worst day of my life." The conversation after he said it would follow a pattern similar to the one above, ending at a seeming impasse. No visible progress.

Until one day, *two years later*, he was coloring a Pokémon picture and said out of nowhere, "I don't really mean that it's the worst day of my life when I say that. I just get mad sometimes."

FOR REAL! That was a massive mom-win for me. I hope you see it as a win for you too. Because most of the time when we attempt to impart really awesome wisdom and coaching to our little wild boys, it looks like nothing is sinking in. But don't let appearances fool you. Seeds are being planted, and they are sprouting under the surface.

My boy still occasionally busts out this phrase when everything is world-endingly horrible. Like, for example, if he isn't allowed to eat a second ice cream sundae. But I take heart knowing that there is so much growth happening, even when I can't see it.

If most of your attempts to walk your son through emotional regulation and understanding look and feel like failures, welcome to the club! We can rejoice together in knowing that none of our efforts will come up void (Romans 8:28).

GRATITUDE

THANKS A LOT

I give you thanks, O LORD, with my whole heart.
—Psalm 138 ESV

Gratitude . . . turns what you have into enough.
—Melody Beattie, *The Language of Letting Go*

We'd just returned home after a walk at a local park. One of my kids (who is not typically oozing with gratitude) took a lap around the kitchen before saying, "Wow. I'm so glad we have a house to live in."

The observation struck me. "Me too!" I said.

"It would be too hard to live outside, but we don't have to. God gave us a house!" this child continued.

"That's right," I said.

I shared this gratitude outburst with my husband, David, later that evening. He told me that while strolling through the park that afternoon, he was describing to this child the things he is grateful for. This turned into a simple prayer. "Thank you, God, for a house to live in," David said. "Thank you for this beautiful place to walk. Thank you for our fun dog, Amy." These simple words stuck in this child's mind, drawing the heart into a place of gratitude that repeated itself internally, and even externally later.

We have the power to build gratitude into our kids' minds and hearts in massive ways. Get this: A study of fourth- and fifth-graders found a relationship between the child's gratitude and his mother's gratitude; but no relationship between the father's gratitude and the child's.[1] Moms have an impact on their kids' gratitude-building.

Studies show that gratitude can combat anxiety, strengthen relationships, and improve mental health.[2] One Italian study found that the more gratitude a person has, the less self-critical and more compassionate he will be.[3] Another study showed that repetitive negative thinking can increase the risk of developing Alzheimer's and dementia, while gratitude may interrupt and displace repetitive negative thinking.[4]

As if the physical benefits weren't compelling enough, God's Word calls us to a heart of thanksgiving to God. (Isn't it funny how we're called to obey something God has commanded, and only learn later *just how good it is for us*?) So many parenting parallels there, huh?

We don't really need convincing that gratitude is important. After all, we are the ones yanking a thanking out of our cute little ingrates, right? "What do you saaaay?"

Did you know that girls are more likely to express gratitude than boys?[5] Our boys will need a little extra intentionality to develop in this department. One interesting finding from the same secular source: In one study, people assigned to pray for a month reported higher gratitude at the end of that month than people who were assigned to think positive thoughts.[6]

We all *want* our little dude to overflow with gratitude—to God, to us, to his teachers. How many times has this happened: As you

> What we're aiming for here isn't simply a parroting of thanks but a **heart** of gratitude. That must come from the inside.

drop your son at Grandma's or a playdate, you stare deeply into his eyeballs and with searing exhortation you tell him, "Don't forget to say 'thank you,' okay? Got it? Practice! 'Thank you for the snack, Grandma.' Don't forget, okay?" If we could shake and talk our boys into valuing gratitude, we'd have accomplished the task thirty times over by now. Alas, what we're aiming for here isn't simply a parroting of thanks but a *heart* of gratitude. That must come from the inside. Thankfully, research shows that we can absolutely cultivate and encourage gratitude in the hearts of our sons. Let's get specific.

HE WILL FOLLOW YOUR LEAD

Say it. Gratitude is contagious. Every time you express thanksgiving for *anything*, you are depositing seeds of thanksgiving into his heart. "Mom always thanks God when she points out a pretty sunset. Huh." Before you know it, he's looking for beautiful sunsets himself, and responding with his own gratitude. My dad would often verbally cherish ordinary moments, like weekend mornings of bed heads and bowls of Cheerios. He'd put an arm around one of his kids and say, "Thank you, Lord, for these kids, for a warm home, for good sleep." I never responded, but I always noticed. The same is true for our boys.

When you are genuinely appreciative of something—anything—say so. Incredible customer service at Chick-fil-A? Ask to speak to the manager, and compliment the staff in front of your kids. Grateful your favorite '90s song that had fallen out of memory just popped on the radio? Say so. Not in a weirdo, obnoxious way. But if you think about something you're thankful for anyway, just go the extra step of saying it aloud. Easy to do, and great seeds to plant.

Gratitude check-in. You know what is loud and sometimes tumultuous? When six hungry kids pile into a minivan at 3:10 p.m. after a seven-hour school day. Car rides home can quickly go south. Whether your car rides are already peaceful, or if you're like me, realizing that shouting "Serenity now!" isn't working, here is a tool to get everyone back on track. Ask your kids to name three things they are grateful for. You take a turn too. Keep repeating the exercise until order has been restored. (Ignore smart-aleck replies, moving on to the next child.) You could also do this at dinnertime or in the morning before school.

Story. Read aloud to your son, or give him a stack of library books to peruse himself. Here are a few we have read that specifically evoke gratitude.

The Thank You Book by Mary Lyn Ray

Town Mouse Country Mouse by Jan Brett

The Book of Virtues by William J Bennett (Probably more of a read-aloud for your younger ones.)

An Old-Fashioned Thanksgiving by Louisa May Alcott

I Will Rejoice by Karma Wilson

Write a thank-you note, draw a picture, or send a video or voice memo. Did Grandma take little Leopold to lunch? Prompt him to draw her a picture of gratitude or write a letter. Did he enjoy his playdate with a classmate? Send a voice text from him and you to the mom who hosted. Simple, genuine, easy.

Keep a gratitude list or whiteboard in the kitchen, and let him add to it. Studies have shown that keeping track of specific things you're grateful for increases happiness and improves mood.

Mental subtraction. "Imagine what life would be like, if [insert positive event or facet of life] had never happened." This is a thought and conversation exercise that researchers call the "George Bailey effect" after the movie *It's a Wonderful Life*. You can start this with your kids in the car or over dinner. "Imagine if we never got our dog, Amy. What would life be like without her?" or "What if we didn't have a house to live in?" Imagine aloud all the things you'd miss out on without it.

Nonmaterial gifts. A lot of parents are moving toward gifting "experiences" instead of material gifts for kids. The making of family memories and reducing toy clutter are wins for mom. But get this—one study showed that people express more gratitude after an experience purchase than after a material-good purchase.[7] So if you want your kids to have more gratitude for gifts, consider experiences in lieu of toys.

BOTTOM LINE

Gratitude is a path to peace, whether we're starting from a peak or a valley. Help your boy to forge this path in his younger years, and he will return to that same path as he grows. Gratitude is a path that ultimately walks us back to the origin of all things, our Creator. Don't discount your smallest deposits of gratitude into the heart of your son. Every word is leading him back to that path. You do good work, mama.

REST

SLEEP? ISN'T THERE AN APP FOR THAT?

Come to me, all you who are weary and burdened, and I will give you rest. Take my yoke upon you and learn from me, for I am gentle and humble in heart, and you will find rest for your souls.

—Matthew 11:28–29 NIrv

If you were to ask me what the single biggest obstacle is for kids to achieve good sleep, it would be entertainment technology.

—Dr. W. Chris Winter, MD, board-certified sleep medicine specialist and neurologist, *The Rested Child*

Practicing what I preach is important to me. That's why I made sure to take a nice long nap before writing this chapter. And to revisit a fun Louie Giglio quote I read on Instagram: "God did more on your behalf while you were sleeping last night than you will do on your behalf while awake today."[1] Just reading the sentence felt like someone wrapped me in a blanket and turned on the lullaby music.

There are two aspects of rest I wanted to cover in this last chapter. The first is the physical rest that human bodies need. God literally commands us to rest one day per week. He made that day specifically for us human people who need to take a rest from the hustle, for crying out loud. It's for our good. Our boys need adequate sleep and downtime. I'm not talking about the kind of numbing-out sedentary state where boys are locked onto their screens, gaming their lives away. Even though they're sitting still, kids simply don't get restorative rest and recreation through their devices. Let's stop fooling ourselves by pretending that when Blayden sits beside you tapping a screen, he is at rest. In reality, his brain is surging in cortisol (the stress hormone) and adrenaline. He is experiencing dopamine surges that lead to device addiction. Plus, too much time on the device will actually hinder Blayden's ability to fall asleep later. In its most basic sense, rest is often diminished. But that very rest is deeply necessary and an underappreciated cause of many of our sons' behavioral challenges today.

The second kind of rest I wanted to cover is heart rest. The kind that feels like a tiny alcove of peace in chaos. Interestingly, we find both the physical rest and the heart rest through Sabbathing. (His commands really are for our good!) It was important to me to end this book with an emphasis on rest. On a bad day, I strive my guts out to do all the best things for my kids, inevitably blow it somewhere along the way, and then resemble an overcaffeinated Jessi Spano, collapsing into a pit of despair. That usually happens when my heart isn't resting in the Father. This kind of rest is a practice we moms desperately need, especially after reading a book listing out all these things your son needs from you with a clock ticking until he turns ten. Yikes! In a minute, we'll talk about how to live our days from rest, and how to pass this on to our sons.

PHYSICAL REST

Marissa's son Cletus never was a great sleeper. But by the time he was six years old, she'd hoped he'd be clocking a full night's sleep. "He'd wake up ready to party at 3 a.m., daily. I couldn't figure out why. We tried everything." Cletus also struggled at school with focus, hyperactivity, and impulsivity. As a result, mom asked his school to test for learning disabilities. Soon after, Marissa noticed Cletus snoring at night, so she mentioned it to his pediatrician. The doctor said that while sleep apnea was rare in kids, a sleep study could rule it out. The doctor called Marissa after the study. "Mild sleep apnea means you stop breathing 0–5 times per hour. Cletus has moderate to severe sleep apnea—he stops breathing 26 times per hour during the night." Marissa sought treatment for her son's sleep apnea and is hopeful that this will also help address his daytime behavioral and attentional struggles.

Did you know that 75 percent of children struggling with mental health issues also have a sleep disorder?[2] Sleep expert and neurologist W. Chris Winter says that oftentimes a sleep disorder is "contributing to (or masquerading as) the psychiatric problem."[3] Too many of our kids are not getting adequate sleep, and the consequences are dire. Dr. Winter writes that sleep disorders are to blame for "epidemic levels of childhood obesity, diabetes, learning and attention disorders, and more mysterious pain and fatigue maladies in children."[4]

According to a study led by a Harvard pediatrician, "children ages 3 to 7 who don't get enough sleep are more likely to have problems with attention, emotional control, and peer relationships in mid-childhood."[5]

I know, like we needed more pressure for our kids to sleep, right? But this research is actually encouraging. Because the solution to poor sleep is pretty simple, according to Dr. Winter. Also, your son's wild ways could possibly be addressed by increasing downtime, without the need for medication. This is good news.

Let's talk sleep basics for a minute, before getting into the kind of long-term soul-style rest that our boys need just as much.

HOW TO BOLSTER YOUR SON'S SLEEP

According to the National Sleep Foundation recommendations, one- to two-year-olds need eleven to fourteen hours of sleep, three- to five-year-olds need ten to thirteen hours of sleep, and six- to thirteen-year-olds need nine to eleven hours of sleep.[6]

All of my kids slept through the night (eight hours without waking) by twelve weeks. We used a book called *On Becoming Babywise*, which I know is controversial in some circles. The main idea is to get your child on a schedule. For my kids, the methods were approached with plenty of love and affection throughout the day, and common sense for when to intervene when baby is crying at night. The basic concept of giving our child the gift of a full night's rest is a blessing to the entire family.

What about beyond the newborn years? Once your child is older, what can you do to help his sleep quantity and quality? If you want to delve deeper into this subject, I recommend grabbing *The Rested Child* by W. Chris Winter, MD. Or check out the *1000 Hours Outside Podcast* episode with Dr. Winter.

Here are two key problems that could be interfering with your son's sleep.

Interactive screen time (like tablets, video games, phone games) played during the day delays a child's ability to fall asleep at night. There are a few reasons for this, but let's address the lighting reason first. If you've bought lightbulbs in the last several years, you know that measuring light is more complex than simply wattage. Lumens measure the potential light output of a bulb. A 40-watt bulb = 450 lumens. A 100-watt bulb = 1,600 lumens. A measurement of light I learned through *The Rested Child* is a lux. Lux is a measure of light exposure. (Or basically, light intensity.) One lux = one lumen per square meter. A bulb's lumens don't change, but if you measured the lux (light exposure) from where you are standing, that would change depending on your distance from the light source. "Studies have shown that LED light sources of 2,000 lux or more to be effective in promoting wakefulness."[7]

More lux promotes more wakefulness. But how few lux can disturb sleep? Get this: Light amounts as low as 5 to 10 lux can disrupt sleep. *This is the light level of a phone on night mode.*[8] So we know the light from our kids' devices can disrupt sleep.

Do you know what else disrupts sleep? Dopamine. Dopamine is the feel-good neurotransmitter released naturally when our brains experience anything enjoyable. As our natural, healthy wake-and-sleep rhythm winds down toward the end of the day, the dopamine in our system declines. That helps us get sleepy. Anything pleasurable we experience can release dopamine, but do you know what cranks up dopamine to artificially high levels? Digital entertainment. If your son is playing on his tablet, Nintendo Switch, an app on your phone, or whatever—his dopamine levels are soaring, exactly at the time you want those levels to be declining.

Do your kids a massive favor by creating healthy and wise parameters around digital entertainment. I say this after having allowed *lots* of gaming for my older kids, course-correcting, and then doing better. Giving your son the tools he needs to get a good night's sleep is critical, uncommon, and it's your job.

After I removed interactive digital entertainment from my children's daily schedule a few years ago, many behavioral struggles vanished. (Not all, of course, as they are still human.) But I didn't realize how profoundly digital entertainment was impacting them, not solely during and after play, but around the clock. Their sleep quality and quantity had been diminished, which manifested as grumpy, ornery behavior during the day, which, on occasion, I didn't want to deal with, so I would allow *more screen time*. The cycle would repeat, until we removed the devices and fixed a host of problems in the process. (The problems were more pronounced for my sons than my daughters.)

> If you want to instantly improve your son's sleep
> quality and quantity, consider a technology break.

If you want to instantly improve your son's sleep quality and quantity, consider a technology break. I know this sounds scary, but I show you exactly how to do this in my book *Digital Detox: The Two-Week Tech Reset for Kids*.

Your son's growing body needs high-quality sleep to function best. In order for you and your marriage to function best, you also need him to sleep.

INTRODUCE HIM TO DEEPER REST FOR HIS SOUL

Just as our bodies need sleep, our souls need rest! I've talked a lot about how distorted our life pace is. Over the last hundred years or so, we've benefitted from many technological advancements: washing machines, dryers, air conditioning, cars, planes, a computer in our pockets. The only problem is that instead of using our extra time to enjoy our family, rest, etc., we stack our schedules a mile high. Our hurried hearts want to scream.

Then this weird lady with six kids and nearly a dozen pets tells you that you have to do these eight things for your son before his tenth birthday. It's important! He needs you! And your heart flips out a little more. Here is the great striving and resting paradox.

Imagine, for a moment, that you are a farmhand. You follow directions the Farmer gives you. You till the land, you plant seeds, you protect against pests and weeds. You want to grow great crops. You want to please your boss. So you work your tail off. You know that your Farmer boss is pleased with your diligence; He is pleased when you follow His expert instructions. He is honored when you tend the seeds as if you owned them yourself. But, at the end of the day, you do not own the land, you do not own the seeds. Some of these seeds will sprout into fruitful crops. Others will stubbornly sprout, seemingly unresponsive to tender care. You, ultimately, cannot control which seed is which. But your Farmer boss does not assess the job you do by that which you cannot control. He is pleased with your heart to work for Him, and He alone owns the outcome. So the farmhand can rest in a job well done, leaving the ultimate results up to the Farmer.

This is the only path to find rest: faith in the One who orchestrates and controls all things. It is the only path to that comfy alcove of rest amidst our high calling and daily chaos. And you can find it anytime. But it takes practice. We moms must remind ourselves that we have access to this rest, or else we will burn out. I know I am deeply prone to be a farmhand who is panicked, running about the field, fretting over not enough rain, or too much wind, or all the other things far outside my control. The only way for my heart to gain rest is to trust the One who controls all the details. And I speak this from a place of experience, my friend.

Let's bring the analogy away from the farm and closer to home. No matter our own circumstances, we can seek and find rest:

- When the therapists tell you they see signs of severe learning disabilities in your two-year-old.
- When your five-year-old talks back to the teacher.
- When you had to call poison control twice—in the same day—because your toddler decided to drink dish soap.
- When one of your kids bears the kind of fruit that makes you certain that you're a phenomenal parent—but their sibling makes you wonder if you are the worst mom of all time.
- When you're exhausted but your little chatterbox will not stop talking about his favorite Pokémon card, for the love of Pete.
- When you attempt family devotional time, and your son uses his actual Bible as a weapon to beat his sister over the head.

When spit hits the fan, we can still find rest. In fact, we can find rest *only* when we remember that the same God who spoke the world into existence has entrusted YOU with the details of your son's life in this season. So many moms I know feel downtrodden and even ashamed as they parent very difficult kids. But guess what? Last I checked, army commanders call their most competent men to the toughest battles. CEOs assign their top dogs to the most complex business matters. And the God of the universe chose you, out of all of the moms on earth throughout time, to parent your wild hooligan. What does that say about you? You are called to this job with exactly the skills you have.

Despite the stigma around striving, we can and will strive in the godliest of ways. We look for opportunities to shape the hearts of our growing boys. We refuse to check out, leaving them to their own devices. Then, we will rest in knowing that God did not call us to be concerned with that which is above our pay grade. He called us to trust Him and do the good works that he prepared in advance for us to do.[9] What does that look like in real life?

When I'm in a terrible parenting pickle, in the midst of the impossible, I audibly say, "I trust you, God." "I don't know how you'll make good out of this, but I know you will." "You are in control, and I am not." "I work for you."

As you live out this kind of resting in the Lord, your son sees it. The testimony of your life witnesses to your boy in ways you cannot imagine. And as he grows, he will learn to wait expectantly, watching for the Lord's work, even while he rests.

Share examples of rest with your son. Do you have a time when you worked your tail off, and then stopped to trust and rest in the Lord? Share the specifics with your son. My boys are often more impressed with random personal stories of experiencing God in real life than they are with my Bible lectures. Just this week I told them how God looked out for me by blocking my plans over and over again. Only later did I understand why His plans were better. So I trust Him, over and over again. I rest in knowing that He always works it all out for my good and His glory. And I drop little breadcrumbs of my faith lived out along the way.

SHOW HIM

Wherever these pages find you, my prayer for you is that you meet your mothering challenges, stress, and difficulties with a heart that chooses to rest in the God amidst your biggest and smallest troubles. When you or your son faces setbacks and frustration, my hope is that you are able to respond, "Sounds like an opportunity for us to trust God, and rest in His promises."

Never underestimate the eternal impact of a godly mom who strives in godliness, rests in God's goodness, and prays for change in the heart of her son.

CONCLUDING THOUGHTS

There's a scene in *Lord of the Rings* in which a selfish and cowardly leader is feeling downtrodden due to his own military missteps. Rather than leading his troops to fight off oppressive enemy forces, he succumbs to his fears, shrinks into a room, and eats a bunch of snacks. He finally emerges from his cocoon of self-pity to see that enemy forces have surrounded the castle. He shouts to his troops, "Abandon your post! Flee!!"[1] (Worst leader ever.)

Thankfully, the wise and valiant Gandalf steps in, bops him on the head, and shouts to the troops, "Prepare for battle!"[2] The troops listen. Despite the bleak situation, the good guys eventually win. (I just saved you three hours.)

Ladies, we are in a war for the hearts of our boys. The landscape is bleak: gaming, toxic messaging that vilifies masculinity, a culture increasingly hostile to God and His Word. This is the world we are raising boys in. We are tempted to give up the fight. But we mustn't.

The God of the universe gives believers His very Spirit—the same Spirit that raised Jesus from death to life—to live in us.[3] Why would we despair? Why would we give up when we have access like this?

I hope you put down this book feeling encouraged, invigorated, and hopeful.

I hope you feel seen in your hardest parenting days. You are SO not alone.

I hope you join me in trusting that God assigns His best soldiers to the toughest battles.

I hope you continue to have faith that the God who made you, who loves you and loves your son, can make a beautiful story out of a pile of muck. Trust Him. Prepare for battle.

ACKNOWLEDGMENTS

This book would not have been written without my husband, David, who supports, encourages, and edits for me. David, you are the wind beneath my wings, and I'm unspeakably grateful for you. Thank you for always making the space for my writing, even when it means a bottleneck in the laundry situation. You are the best.

Thank you to my three sons, who challenge and humble me on a daily basis. Jack, Carter, and Mason: You make me laugh and you make my eye twitch like no one else. God sure blessed me with you three. Now go clean your rooms.

Thank you, Cynthia, you are a treasure of a human and a wonderful literary agent.

Thank you, Jennifer, you are one of a kind—editor, writer, communicator. You make all projects so much better.

Thank you, Sharon, for lending your keen eye to this book.

Thank you to my dear friends who read, gave feedback, and generously shared their own stories that went into the book: Melissa, Caitlin, Cayla, Candice, Ashley G., Ashley P., Tina, Marissa, Rhonda, Nancy.

Thank you, Kuppa Joy, for great coffee in a bright space with good music. I wrote so many of these pages in your shop.

Thank you, reader, for the time you spent with me in these pages. I hope you found them useful and encouraging.

Thank you, Lord, for your wisdom, your Word, your truth to ground me when everything feels hard. Thank you for loving my kids more than I ever could, and for entrusting them to me as their mom.

NOTES

Introduction

1. George R. Barna, "*American Worldview Inventory 2020*: Final Release #12, Restoring America by Reframing Its Worldview" (November 2020): 2.

2. Genesis 6.

3. 1 Samuel 17.

4. 1 Samuel 24.

5. Ruth 2.

6. 2 Thessalonians 3:8.

7. Matthew 20:28.

8. TED: The Economics Daily, Bureau of Labor Statistics, "How Parents Used Their Time in 2021," July 22, 2022, https://www.bls.gov/opub/ted/2022/how-par ents-used-their-time-in-2021.htm.

9. Jill Anderson, "A Crisis of Belonging," *Harvard Graduate School of Education Edcast,* March 2023, https://www.gse.harvard.edu/ideas/edcast/23/03/crisis -belonging.

10. Jean Guerrero, citing Equimundo "State of American Men" report, in "Why Are Men So Lonely?," *Los Angeles Times,* January 15, 2024, https://www.latimes .com/opinion/story/2024-01-15/men-friendship-gen-z-loneliness.

11. Ecclesiastes 12:13.

12. Deborah Serani, "The Benefits of Humor," *Psychology Today,* April 2022. https://www.psychologytoday.com/us/blog/two-takes-depression/202204/the -benefits-humor.

13. "The Common Sense Census: Media Use by Tweens and Teens, 2021," *Common Sense Media,* https://www.commonsensemedia.org/research/the-common -sense-census-media-use-by-tweens-and-teens-2021.

Chapter 1 Value

1. John Newton, *The Works of the Rev. John Newton,* vol. 1 (New York: Robert Carter, 1844), 7.

2. Newton, *Works,* 81.

Chapter 2 Purpose

1. Stephen King, *On Writing: A Memoir of the Craft* (New York: Scribner, 2010), 29.

2. Warren Farrell, "'Boy Crisis' Threatens America's Future with Economic, Health and Suicide Risks," *USA Today*, April 7, 2019, https://www.usatoday.com/story/opinion/2019/04/07/males-risk-boy-crisis-identity-america-future-addiction-suicide-column/3331366002/.

3. Richard V. Reeves and Ember Smith, "Commentary: The Male College Crisis Is Not Just in Enrollment, But Completion," *Brookings*, October 8, 2021, https://www.brookings.edu/articles/the-male-college-crisis-is-not-just-in-enrollment-but-completion/.

4. Josh Shipp, "Your Child's Most Annoying Trait May Just Reveal Their Greatest Strengths," TEDx Talk, October 18, 2017, https://www.youtube.com/watch?v=mU5WO93Kw4E.

5. Matthew 16:21–23.

6. John 21:4–7.

Chapter 3 Family Dinner

1. Jill Anderson, "The Benefit of Family Mealtime," *Harvard Graduate School of Education EdCast*, April 1, 2020, https://www.gse.harvard.edu/ideas/edcast/20/04/benefit-family-mealtime.

2. Anderson, "The Benefit of Family Mealtime."

Part 2 Relationship

1. Liz Mineo, "Good Genes Are Nice, But Joy Is Better," *Harvard Gazette*, April 11, 2017, https://news.harvard.edu/gazette/story/2017/04/over-nearly-80-years-harvard-study-has-been-showing-how-to-live-a-healthy-and-happy-life/.

2. Mineo, "Good Genes Are Nice."

Chapter 4 Eye Contact

1. Mandy Len Catron, "To Fall in Love with Anyone, Do This," *New York Times*, January 11, 2015, https://www.nytimes.com/2015/01/11/style/modern-love-to-fall-in-love-with-anyone-do-this.html.

2. Catron, "To Fall in Love."

3. Catron, "To Fall in Love."

4. Brian Grazer, *Face to Face: The Art of Human Connection* (New York: Simon & Schuster, 2019), 9.

5. Lydia Denworth, "Hyperscans Show How Brains Sync as People Interact," *Scientific American*, April 10, 2019, https://www.scientificamerican.com/article/hyperscans-show-how-brains-sync-as-people-interact/.

6. Susan Pinker, *The Village Effect: How Face-to-Face Contact Can Make Us Healthier and Happier* (Toronto: Vintage Canada, 2015), 125.

7. Michael Kramer, quoted in Pinker, *The Village Effect*, 132. I don't know if there's a more controversial topic than breastfeeding. This is one perspective. ☺

8. "The Common Sense Census: Media Use by Tweens and Teens, 2021," March 9, 2022, https://www.commonsensemedia.org/research/the-common-sense-cens us-media-use-by-tweens-and-teens-2021.

Chapter 5 Conversation

1. Anne Trafton, "Back-and-Forth Exchanges Boost Children's Brain Response to Language," *MIT News*, February 13, 2018, https://news.mit.edu/2018/conversation -boost-childrens-brain-response-language-0214.

2. Dana Suskind, *Thirty Million Words: Building a Child's Brain* (New York City: Dutton, 2015), 34, 37.

3. Susan Pinker, *The Village Effect: How Face-to-Face Contact Can Make Us Healthier and Happier* (Toronto: Vintage Canada, 2015), 126.

4. Sherry Turkle, "Stop Googling. Let's Talk.," *New York Times*, September 26, 2015, https://www.nytimes.com/2015/09/27/opinion/sunday/stop-googling-lets -talk.html?searchResultPosition=1.

5. Turkle, "Stop Googling."

Chapter 6 Conflict

1. Ralph Waldo Emerson, *Conduct of Life*, selected digitized books, Library of Congress (Boston: Houghton Mifflin and Company, 1888), 16, https://www.loc .gov/resource/gdcmassbookdig.conductoflife00emer_0/?sp=22&r=-0.356,0.368 ,1.682,0.761,0

2. Chip Ingram, "Forgiving—How to Restore Your Peace" message transcript, *Living on the Edge with Chip Ingram*, n.d., https://livingontheedge.org/broadcast/for giving-how-to-restore-your-peace/?srsltid=AfmBOoq_LPe4Z4JUaXQWZG6P6 EQ-sfqDvb5xYtvhOKnNCp6TyLizl0y3.

Chapter 7 Self-Forgetfulness

1. John Bartlett, *Familiar Quotations*, 14th ed. (Boston: Little, Brown and Company, 1968), 1007.

2. Leonie Helm, "Adult Child Still Living at Home? How to Spot Failure to Launch Syndrome," *Newsweek*, January 2023, https://www.newsweek.com/failure -launch-syndrome-adult-children-parenting-1762310.

3. Vasilis K. Pozios, Praveen R. Kambam, and H. Eric Bender, "Does Media Violence Lead to the Real Thing?" *New York Times*, August 23, 2013, https://www.nytimes .com/2013/08/25/opinion/sunday/does-media-violence-lead-to-the-real-thing.html.

4. Leonard Sax, *Boys Adrift: The Five Factors Driving the Growing Epidemic of Unmotivated Boys and Underachieving Young Men* (New York: Basic Books, 2016), 64–65.

5. Sax, *Boys Adrift*, 65.

Chapter 8 Respecting Authority

1. Timothy Keller, quoted in Bret Eckelberry, "Honor Your Father and Mother," *Focus on the Family*, March 8, 2024, https://www.focusonthefamily.com/live-it-post /honor-your-father-and-mother/.

2. Hebrews 10:25.

Chapter 9 Natural Consequences

1. Travis Hellstrom, *The Abraham Lincoln Book of Quotes* (New York: Hatherleigh, 2023), 21.

2. Angela Duckworth, "Self-Discipline Outdoes IQ in Predicting Academic Performance of Adolescents," *National Library of Medicine*, December 2005, https://pubmed.ncbi.nlm.nih.gov/16313657/.

3. Terrie Moffitt, Richie Poulton, and Avshalom Caspi, "Lifelong Impact of Early Self-Control," *American Scientist*, September-October 2013, https://www.americanscientist.org/article/lifelong-impact-of-early-self-control.

Chapter 10 Waiting

1. John Anderer, "Hurry Up! Modern Patience Thresholds Lower Than Ever Before, Technology to Blame," *Study Finds*, September 2019, https://studyfinds.org/hurry-up-modern-patience-thresholds-lower-than-ever-before-survey-finds/.

2. Timothy Keller, *The Freedom of Self Forgetfulness: The Path to True Christian Joy* (Leyland, England: 10Publishing, 2012).

3. 1 Samuel 13:14; Acts 13:22.

4. G. Michael Hopf, *Those Who Remain: A Post-Apocalyptic Novel* (United States: G. Michael Hopf, 2016), 18.

5. Genesis 25:29–34. It was actually lentil soup and a chunk of bread!

Chapter 11 Humor

1. Dexter Louie et al., "The Laughter Prescription: A Tool for Lifestyle Mediation," *American Journal of Lifestyle Medicine* 10, no. 4 (2016): 262–267, https://www.ncbi.nlm.nih.gov/pmc/articles/PMC6125057/.

2. Louie et al., "Laughter Prescription."

3. Deborah Serani, "The Benefits of Humor," *Psychology Today*, April 25, 2022. https://www.psychologytoday.com/us/blog/two-takes-depression/202204/the-benefits-humor.

4. Jill Suttie, "How Laughter Brings Us Together," *Greater Good Magazine*, July 17, 2017, https://greatergood.berkeley.edu/article/item/how_laughter_brings_us_together.

5. Serani, "The Benefits of Humor."

6. Brandan M. Savage et al., "Humor, Laughter, Learning and Health! A Brief Review," *Advances in Physiology Education* 41, no. 3 (July 2017): 341–347, https://journals.physiology.org/doi/full/10.1152/advan.00030.2017.

7. Judith Warner, "The Kids Aren't Alright. Are Phones Really to Blame?" *Washington Post*, March 22, 2024, https://www.washingtonpost.com/books/2024/03/22/anxious-generation-rewiring-childhood-jonathan-haidt-review/.

8. Jonathan Haidt et al., *What Is Happening to Boys: A Collaborative Review*, unpublished manuscript, New York University, n.d., 17, https://docs.google.com/document/d/1Fcio_tkbnNkmCi1nsHGiTLinFqdLJJlAtCzmec-Ss4s/edit (Fatal Injury Reports, National, Regional and State, 1981–2020. *Centers for Disease Control and Prevention*, https://wisqars.cdc.gov/fatal-reports).

Chapter 12 Tedious Responsibilities

1. John Bartlett, *Familiar Quotations*, 14th ed. (Boston: Little, Brown and Company, 1968), 98.

2. Findings by University of Minnesota researcher Marty Rossman cited in Susan Newman, "Best Age for Kids to Start Doing Chores," *Psychology Today*, November 21, 2022, https://www.psychologytoday.com/us/blog/singletons/202211/best-age -kids-start-doing-chores.

3. Elizabeth M. White et al., "Associations Between Household Chores and Childhood Self-Competency," *Journal of Developmental & Behavioral Pediatrics* 40, no. 3 (April 2019): 176–182, https://journals.lww.com/jrnldbp/abstract/2019 /04000/associations_between_household_chores_and.3.aspx.

Part 5 Bravery

1. R. Meredith Elkins, quoted in Alvin Powell, "Building 'Bravery Muscles' to Fight Rising Anxiety Among Kids," *Harvard Gazette*, October 7, 2022, https://news.harvard .edu/gazette/story/2022/10/building-bravery-muscles-to-fight-rising-youth-anxiety/.

Chapter 13 Failure

1. "5 Things to Know: Surprising Facts About Martin Luther King Jr.," *Smithsonian's National Museum of African American History and Culture*, n.d., https://nmaahc .si.edu/explore/stories/5-things-know-surprising-facts.

2. Yvonne Villarreal, "A New Home for Budding Filmmakers at USC," *Los Angeles Times*, March 30, 2009, https://www.latimes.com/archives/la-xpm-2009-mar-30 -et-lucas30-story.html.

3. "'You've Got to Find What You Love,' Jobs Says" (prepared text of Stanford University commencement address), *Stanford Report*, June 12, 2005, https://news .stanford.edu/2005/06/12/youve-got-find-love-jobs-says/.

Chapter 14 Risk

1. Jonathan Haidt, *The Anxious Generation: How the Great Rewiring of Childhood Is Causing an Epidemic of Mental Illness* (New York: Penguin, 2024), 62.

2. Haidt, *The Anxious Generation*, 75.

3. Haidt, *The Anxious Generation*, 75.

4. Liz Mineo, "Good Genes Are Nice, But Joy Is Better," *Harvard Gazette*, April 11, 2017, https://news.harvard.edu/gazette/story/2017/04/over-nearly-80-years -harvard-study-has-been-showing-how-to-live-a-healthy-and-happy-life/.

5. Ben Woelk, "Wind, Trees, and Security Awareness," *Educause Review*, September 13, 2019, https://er.educause.edu/blogs/2019/9/wind-trees-and-security-awareness.

6. Woelk, "Wind, Trees, and Security Awareness."

7. Haidt, *The Anxious Generation*, 67.

Chapter 15 Grit

1. Angela Duckworth, "Research," *Angela Duckworth*, 2024, https://angeladuc kworth.com/research/.

2. Julie Jargon, "Boys Are Struggling. It Can Take Coaches, Tutors and Thousands a Month to Fix That," *Wall Street Journal*, December 9, 2023, https://www.wsj.com/tech/personal-tech/middle-schoolers-academic-success-innovation-40e8456d.

3. Jargon, "Boys Are Struggling."

4. 1 Timothy 4:7–8 ESV.

5. See Matthew 7:14; John 16:33.

6. Bodie Hodge, "How Long Did It Take for Noah to Build the Ark," *Answers in Genesis*, 2024, https://answersingenesis.org/bible-timeline/how-long-did-it-take-for-noah-to-build-the-ark/.

Chapter 16 Wonder

1. Sally Clarkson, *Awaking Wonder: Opening Your Child's Heart to the Beauty of Learning* (Minneapolis: Bethany House, 2020), 14.

2. G. K. Chesterton, *Tremendous Trifles* (New York: Dodd, Mead and Company, 1909), 7.

3. Clarkson, *Awaking Wonder*, 39.

4. John 4:24.

5. "Petty Officer Second Class (SEAL) Michael A. Monsoor: For Actions on Sept. 29, 2006," U.S. Navy, Medal of Honor Recipients, https://www.navy.mil/medal-of-honor-recipient-michael-a-monsoor/.

6. John 15:13 NIrV.

Chapter 17 Accurate Appraisal of Self

1. Rev. J. Wilbur Chapman, *The Life and Work of Dwight L. Moody* (Chicago: International Publishing Co., 1900), 72.

2. See Romans 3:23.

3. Proverbs 27:2 ESV.

4. Michelle Brandt, "Video Games Activate Reward Regions of Brain in Men More Than Women, Stanford Study Finds," *Stanford Medicine*, February 4, 2008, https://med.stanford.edu/news/all-news/2008/02/video-games-activate-reward-regions-of-brain-in-men-more-than-women-stanford-study-finds.html.

5. Sean Parker, quoted in Mike Allen, "Sean Parker Unloads on Facebook: 'God Only Knows What It's Doing to Our Children's Brains,'" *Axios*, November 9, 2017, www.axios.com/2017/12/15/sean-parker-unloads-on-facebook-god-only-knows-what-its-doing-to-our-childrens-brains-1513306792.

6. Parker in Allen, "Sean Parker Unloads."

Chapter 18 Grace

1. Tim Challies, *Devoted: Great Men and Their Godly Moms* (Minneapolis: Cruciform, 2018), 93.

2. John Newton, "Amazing Grace," https://www.hymnal.net/en/hymn/h/313.

Chapter 19 Get Outside

1. "Children in Nature: Improving Health by Reconnecting Youth with the Outdoors," *National Recreation and Park Association*, n.d., https://www.nrpa.org /uploadedFiles/nrpa.org/Advocacy/Children-in-Nature.pdf.

2. "The Common Sense Census: Media Use by Tweens and Teens, 2021," *Common Sense*, March 12, 2022, https://www.commonsensemedia.org/research/the -common-sense-census-media-use-by-tweens-and-teens-2021.

3. The term is attributed to University of Maryland professor of kinesiology Jane Clark in Richard Louv, *Last Child in the Woods: Saving Our Children from Nature-Deficit Disorder* (Chapel Hill, NC: Algonquin Books, 2008), 35.

4. Louv, *Last Child in the Woods*, 35.

5. Louv, *Last Child in the Woods*, 50.

6. Louv, *Last Child in the Woods*, 3, 100.

7. Danae Lund, "Top 5 Benefits of Children Playing Outside," *Sanford Health*, June 26, 2018, https://news.sanfordhealth.org/childrens/play-outside/.

8. Lund, "Top 5 Benefits."

9. Lise Eliot, "Brain Differences in Boys and Girls: How Much Is Inborn?" *Scientific American*, March 1, 2016, https://www.scientificamerican.com/article/brain -differences-in-boys-and-girls-how-much-is-inborn/.

10. Claire McCarthy, "6 Reasons Children Need to Play Outside," *Harvard Health Publishing*, October 27, 2020, https://www.health.harvard.edu/blog/6-reasons-chi ldren-need-to-play-outside-2018052213880.

11. "Obesity: Definition and Overview," *The Nutrition Source*, Harvard T. H. Chan School of Public Health, 2024, https://www.hsph.harvard.edu/obesity-prevention -source/obesity-trends-original/global-obesity-trends-in-children/#References.

12. "How Childhood Obesity Rates Have Changed Over Time," State of Childhood Obesity, September 9, 2019, https://stateofchildhoodobesity.org/how-child hood-obesity-rates-have-changed-over-time/.

13. Bindra Shah et al., "Sex and Gender Differences in Childhood Obesity: Contributed to the Research Agenda," *BMJ Nutrition, Prevention & Health* 3, no. 2 (2020): 387–390, https://pmc.ncbi.nlm.nih.gov/articles/PMC7841817/.

Chapter 20 Boredom

1. Linda Rodriguez McRobbie, "The History of Boredom," *Smithsonian Magazine*, November 20, 2012, https://www.smithsonianmag.com/science-nature/the-history -of-boredom-138176427/.

2. Ed Young (@ed_young), Instagram post, January 19, 2024, https://www .instagram.com/ed_young/?hl=en.

3. Dennis Thompson, "Injuries, Burnout Keep Too Many Kids from Sticking with Sports," *U.S. News and World Report*, January 2024, https://www.usnews.com /news/health-news/articles/2024-01-22/injuries-burnout-keep-too-many-kids -from-sticking-with-sports.

4. "AAP Calls Out Causes of Overuse Injuries & Burnout in Youth Sports," January 22, 2024, HealthyChildren.org, https://www.healthychildren.org/English /news/Pages/AAP-calls-out-causes-of-injury-overtraining-and-burnout-in-youth -sports.aspx.

5. Angela Duckworth, *Grit: The Power of Passion and Perseverance* (New York: Scribner, 2016), 104.

Chapter 21 Language for Feelings

1. Dr. Seigel's work is highlighted in Lisa Firestone, "Name It to Tame It: The Emotions Underlying Your Triggers," *Psychology Today*, February 1, 2022.

2. Firestone, "Name It to Tame It."

3. Jean Guerrero, citing Equimundo "State of American Men" report, in "Why Are Men So Lonely?" *Los Angeles Times*, January 15, 2024, https://www.latimes.com/opinion/story/2024-01-15/men-friendship-gen-z-loneliness.

4. Guerrero, "State of American Men."

5. Guerrero, "State of American Men."

6. Guerrero, "State of American Men."

7. Ephesians 5:28–29; 1 Peter 3:7.

8. Greg Lukianoff and Jonathan Haidt, *The Coddling of the American Mind: How Good Intentions and Bad Ideas Are Setting Up a Generation for Failure* (New York: Penguin, 2018), 35.

9. Lukianoff and Haidt, *Coddling of the American Mind*, 36.

10. 2 Corinthians 10:5.

11. Jeremiah 17:9 NASB.

12. Greg Lukianoff and Jonathan Haidt, "The Coddling of the American Mind," *Atlantic*, September 2015. The authors present a partial list from Robert L. Leahy et al., *Treatment Plans and Interventions for Depression and Anxiety Disorders* (New York: Guilford, 2012), 441.

13. You can see Lukianoff and Haidt's full list (culled from Leahy et al.) in a posting of "The Coddling of the American Mind" article on the Foundation for Individual Rights and Expression website, https://www.thefire.org/news/blogs/eternally-radical-idea/coddling-american-mind. A slightly different version is also included in their book, *The Coddling of the American Mind*.

14. Robert L. Leahy et al., *Treatment Plans and Interventions for Depression and Anxiety Disorders* (New York: Guilford, 2012), 441.

15. Leahy et al., *Treatment Plans and Interventions*, 441.

16. Leahy et al., *Treatment Plans and Interventions*, 441.

17. Leahy et al., *Treatment Plans and Interventions*, 441.

Chapter 22 Gratitude

1. Summer Allen, "The Science of Gratitude," *The Greater Good Science Center at UC Berkeley*, May 2018, 4.

2. Najma Khorrami, "Gratitude Helps Curb Anxiety," *Psychology Today*, July 20, 2020.

3. Khorrami, "Gratitude Helps Curb Anxiety."

4. Khorrami, "Gratitude Helps Curb Anxiety."

5. Allen, "Science of Gratitude," 3.

6. Allen, "Science of Gratitude," 4.

7. Allen, "Science of Gratitude," 52.

Chapter 23 Rest

1. Louie Giglio, @louiegiglio, Instagram, https://www.instagram.com/louiegiglio/p/C38CFytrPzr/?img_index=louiegiglio.

2. W. Chris Winter, *The Rested Child: Why Your Tired, Wired, or Irritable Child May Have a Sleep Disorder—and How to Help* (New York: Penguin Random House, 2022), xii.

3. Winter, *The Rested Child*, xii.

4. Winter, *The Rested Child*, xii.

5. Sue McGreevey, "Study Flags Later Risks for Sleep-Deprived Kids," *Harvard Gazette*, March 10, 2017, https://news.harvard.edu/gazette/story/2017/03/study-flags-later-risks-for-sleep-deprived-kids/.

6. Winter, *The Rested Child*, 57.

7. Winter, *The Rested Child*, 174.

8. Winter, *The Rested Child*, 174.

9. See Ephesians 2:10.

Concluding Thoughts

1. Peter Jackson, *The Lord of the Rings: The Return of the King*, New Line Cinema, 2003.

2. Jackson, *The Return of the King*.

3. See Romans 8:11.

MOLLY DeFRANK is a mother to six kids ages eight to fifteen. She is also the author of *Digital Detox: The Two-Week Tech Reset for Kids*. Molly has been featured on numerous outlets including *Fox News*, CBS's *The Doctors*, *1000 Hours Outside Podcast*, *Focus on the Family Podcast*, *Mama Bear Apologetics Podcast*, and many more. Before having kids, she worked for California elected officials including Governor Arnold Schwarzenegger. Molly, her husband, and their kids live in central California, where she enjoys serving as a leader in women's ministry at her local church. Her favorite things include well-prepared food and well-timed puns. She is proud to be fluent in Dad-Joke. Find her online for parenting encouragement, relatable stories, and photos of more pets than any reasonable human being should have.

CONNECT WITH MOLLY:

MollyDefrank.com

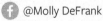 @Molly DeFrank

 @mollydefrank